Alex
Rodriguez

Alex Rodriguez

by Michael V. Uschan

LUCENT BOOKS

A part of Gale, Cengage Learning

Detroit • New York • San Francisco • New Haven, Conn • Waterville, Maine • London

GALE
CENGAGE Learning

LIBRARY OF CONGRESS CATALOGING-IN-PUBLICATION DATA

Uschan, Michael V.
  Alex Rodriguez / by Michael V. Uschan.
    p. cm. -- (People in the news)
  Includes bibliographical references and index.
  ISBN 978-1-4205-0350-0 (hardcover)
  1. Rodriguez, Alex, 1975--Juvenile literature. 2. Baseball players--United States--Biography--Juvenile literature. I. Title.
  GV865.R62U83 2011
  796.357092--dc22
  [B]
                                                                    2010035231

Lucent Books
27500 Drake Rd
Farmington Hills MI 48331

ISBN-13: 978-1-4205-0350-0
ISBN-10: 1-4205-0350-2

Printed in the United States of America
1 2 3 4 5 6 7 14 13 12 11 10

Printed by Bang Printing, Brainerd, MN, 1st Ptg., 01/2011

Contents

Fame and celebrity are alluring. People are drawn to those who walk in fame's spotlight, whether they are known for great accomplishments or for notorious deeds. The lives of the famous pique public interest and attract attention, perhaps because their experiences seem in some ways so different from, yet in other ways so similar to, our own.

Newspapers, magazines, and television regularly capitalize on this fascination with celebrity by running profiles of famous people. For example, television programs such as *Entertainment Tonight* devote all their programming to stories about entertainment and entertainers. Magazines such as *People* fill their pages with stories of the private lives of famous people. Even newspapers, newsmagazines, and television news frequently delve into the lives of well-known personalities. Despite the number of articles and programs, few provide more than a superficial glimpse at their subjects.

Lucent's People in the News series offers young readers a deeper look into the lives of today's newsmakers, the influences that have shaped them, and the impact they have had in their fields of endeavor and on other people's lives. The subjects of the series hail from many disciplines and walks of life. They include authors, musicians, athletes, political leaders, entertainers, entrepreneurs, and others who have made a mark on modern life and who, in many cases, will continue to do so for years to come.

These biographies are more than factual chronicles. Each book emphasizes the contributions, accomplishments, or deeds that have brought fame or notoriety to the individual and shows how that person has influenced modern life. Authors portray their subjects in a realistic, unsentimental light. For example, Bill Gates—the cofounder and chief executive officer of the software giant Microsoft—has been instrumental in making personal computers the most vital tool of the modern age. Few dispute his business savvy, his perseverance, or his technical expertise, yet critics say he is ruthless in his dealings with competitors and driven more by his desire to maintain Microsoft's dominance in the computer industry than by an interest in furthering technology.

In these books, young readers will encounter inspiring stories about real people who achieved success despite enormous obstacles. Oprah Winfrey—the most powerful, most watched, and wealthiest woman on television today—spent the first six years of her life in the care of her grandparents while her unwed mother sought work and a better life elsewhere. Her adolescence was colored by pregnancy at age fourteen, rape, and sexual abuse.

Each author documents and supports his or her work with an array of primary and secondary source quotations taken from diaries, letters, speeches, and interviews. All quotes are footnoted to show readers exactly how and where biographers derive their information and provide guidance for further research. The quotations enliven the text by giving readers eyewitness views of the life and accomplishments of each person covered in the People in the News series.

In addition, each book in the series includes photographs, annotated bibliographies, timelines, and comprehensive indexes. For both the casual reader and the student researcher, the People in the News series offers insight into the lives of today's newsmakers—people who shape the way we live, work, and play in the modern age.

A Controversial Superstar

In 1996, the first year Alex Rodriguez played an entire season of baseball at the major league level for the Seattle Mariners, his teammates noticed that the young man marked his uniforms and equipment "A-ROD." They quickly began calling him by that name. Dave Niehaus, the radio announcer for the Mariners' games, liked the nickname so much that he began calling Rodriguez "A-Rod" during games. "It just seemed natural to me. And it stuck like glue,"[1] says Niehaus.

Since 1996, Rodriguez's nickname has become instantly recognizable to millions of people due to his historic feats in baseball. Unfortunately, various controversies have threatened to overshadow his accomplishments as a player.

First Pick

Rodriguez became known to the sports world on June 3, 1993, when the Seattle Mariners made him the first pick in Major League Baseball's annual amateur draft. He played his first major league game the next season, and in 1996 Rodriguez established everlasting fame with a batting average of .358, the highest that season in Major League Baseball's American League and the highest ever for a major league player younger than twenty-one years old when the season began. The impressive season made many people believe that Rodriguez could become one of the greatest players in the history

Baseball player Alex Rodriguez, nicknamed A-Rod, signed a record-breaking contract with the Texas Rangers and went on to be a New York Yankee. Later in his career he revealed that he had taken steroids.

of baseball. Typical of the accolades Rodriguez received was this one by Dan Duquette, general manager of the Boston Red Sox, who said, "The way he's going, someday he might bat .400 and hit 60 home runs. He's the best young talent I've seen in years."[2]

In the next four seasons, Rodriguez lived up to the lofty predictions, and many people began to consider him the best player in the game. Then in 2000, the Texas Rangers signed Rodriguez to a historic contract: a ten-year, $252-million pact that made him the highest-paid player in any sport. The contract's huge size, though, also made him a lightning rod for criticism. It was not his fault that a team wanted to pay him so much money, but many fans and members of the news media held it against him, claiming that no player was worth $20 million a season. When the Rangers struggled for three years, critics accused Rodriguez of not earning his giant salary by helping the team win more games. He suffered through such criticism even though he played well. In 2003 Rodriguez was voted the American League's Most Valuable Player, an incredible accomplishment for a player on a losing team.

The Rangers traded Rodriguez to the New York Yankees in 2004, but he remained a controversial figure in New York because of his huge salary and inability to help the Yankees win a World Series title in his first five seasons with the team. The criticism came even though Rodriguez continued to play better than almost most players and won two more Most Valuable Player awards in 2005 and 2007. Rodriguez finally led the Yankees to the 2009 championship, but that was the same season he became embroiled in the biggest controversy of his career.

In February 2009 *Sports Illustrated* magazine reported that Rodriguez tested positive in 2003 for anabolic steroids, man-made testosterone hormones that are prescribed by doctors to strengthen patients with severe diseases. They are illegal without a prescription. Major League Baseball banned the use of steroids in 1991 because, in addition to causing serious side effects, they help players become stronger, giving them an unfair advantage over their competitors. Even though Rodriguez was only 1 of 104 players who tested positive for steroids in 2003, he took the brunt of criticism because he was the most-famous player named. The news media bashed Rodriguez for cheating by using steroids and claimed their use had tainted his many achievements.

Rodriguez admitted he had used steroids from 2001 to 2003 while with the Texas Rangers. After apologizing to fans and his team for taking steroids, he went on to prove he was a good player without steroids. He did that by having a solid regular season followed by a World Series championship with the Yankees in 2009. Although not everyone forgave Rodriguez, the World Series title and contrite way in which he admitted he had done something wrong helped endear him again to many fans.

History and Controversy

In the ninth inning of a game against the Tampa Bay Rays on October 4, 2009, Rodriguez hit a fly ball off reliever Troy Percival. The towering drive over the left-field foul pole struck the D-Ring catwalk high above Tropicana Field, a domed stadium, and flew into the left-field stands for a home run. When the Rays claimed it was a foul ball, umpire Charlie Reliford viewed the instant replay video to check if it had been fair. After reviewing the disputed hit, Reliford ruled it was fair and a home run.

The homer was Rodriguez's 31st of the season and 549th in his career, and it placed him squarely in twelfth place among home-run leaders of all times. The homer was also historic because it was the first time instant replay was used in a baseball game. Major league officials had approved the use of instant replay video late in the season after a rash of disputed calls, including one on May 21 in which umpires had denied Rodriguez a home run at Yankee Stadium when the ball bounced back onto the field after it hit a set of yellow stairs past the fence in right-center field. After the ruling on October 4, Rodriguez commented, "There's probably 800 players in the big leagues, and the odds of me being involved were probably 2–1. It's funny. Somehow I find myself in those situations all the time. It was just nice to get the right call and get a fair ruling."[3]

Rodriguez laughed when he said that. So did reporters, who knew that A-Rod was simply one of those players who always seemed to be involved in controversy even when he was doing something historic.

Chapter 1

A Difficult Childhood

I n 2007 Alex Rodriguez wrote *Out of the Ballpark*, a picture book for children. The book, based on Rodriguez's own life, tells the tale of a young boy named Alex who helps his team win a baseball championship. In a postscript to the book, Rodriguez tells readers that if they work as hard as he did, they can realize their own dreams. He writes, "It's a fictional story, but it's based on things I actually did—like getting up at 5 A.M. to practice my baseball fundamentals! I have always been a hard worker both on and off the field. No matter what your dreams and goals, you can never go wrong if you give them all you've got."[4]

The book includes many references to Rodriguez's childhood, such as the team Alex plays on (the Caribes), his best friend's nickname name (J.D.), the home run Alex hits over a fence into a nearby swimming pool, and the fact that his dad is not a part of his life. The fictional Alex, just like Rodriguez, finds joy in playing baseball, and the sport becomes the focus of his life while growing up.

Born in New York

Alexander Emmanuel Rodriguez was born on July 27, 1975, in New York City to Victor and Lourdes Rodriguez, immigrants from the Dominican Republic. Although Rodriguez has lived in the United States most of his life, he has always loved the homeland

Alex Rodriguez wrote the children's book Out of the Ballpark *in 2007. He based the story on his own life.*

of his parents. "Deep down, I'm a Dominican," Rodriguez said once. "I grew up in [New York and] Miami, but my roots are Dominican. That's what my parents were from. That's where my loyalty is."[5] Alex's sister, Suzy, is four years older, and his brother, Joe, is six years older. Rodriguez also has a half brother, Victor M. Rodriguez Jr. who was born in 1960 in the Dominican Republic to Alex's father during his first marriage.

Victor and Lourdes Rodriguez moved to the United States in the early 1970s to better themselves financially. Settling in Washington Heights, a neighborhood in New York City, they worked hard to accomplish that goal. Victor operated Victor's Shoes, a shoe store out of the family's small apartment, and Lourdes worked at a nearby General Motors factory. Because

Dominican Baseball Roots

Even though Alex Rodriguez was born in New York City, he feels a strong connection to the Dominican Republic because it is his parents' homeland. It is also where he lived for several years as a child and first began to play baseball.

Osvaldo "Ozzie" Virgil was the first major league player from the Dominican Republic.

The Dominican Republic has a long, storied tradition of baseball, which extends back to the 1890s when people there began playing *béisbol*, the Spanish name for the game that had begun in the United States just a few decades earlier. The game grew in popularity in the Dominican Republic in the first half of the twentieth century.

In 1956 Osvaldo "Ozzie" Virgil became the first player from the Dominican Republic to play in the major leagues. The infielder began his career with the New York Giants and played nine seasons for six different teams. Virgil played so well that major league teams, hungry for new talent, began to sign other players from the Dominican Republic, including brothers Felipe, Matty, and Jesús Alou; Juan Marichal; Manny Mota; and Sammy Sosa. Sosa became a seven-time all-star who in 1998 hit sixty-six home runs. Felipe Alou not only played baseball for seventeen seasons, but on May 22, 1992, he also became the first Dominican-born manager in major league baseball when he was hired by the Montreal Expos. More than five hundred Dominicans have played in the major leagues, including Boston Red Sox star David Ortiz, the player known as "Big Papi" who in 2007 led the Red Sox to a World Series title. The heavy-hitting Ortiz has been named to several all-star teams and holds the Red Sox single-season record for home runs with fifty-four.

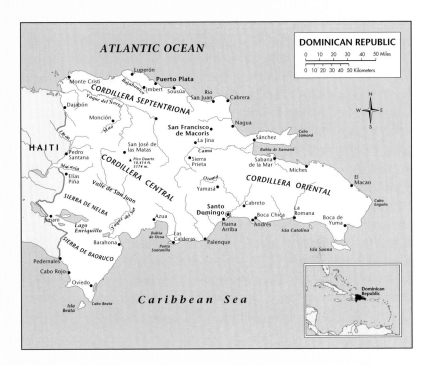

Rodriguez's parents and older siblings were born in the Dominican Republic, a small country south of Florida in the Caribbean Sea.

Lourdes had to leave for work at 4 A.M. every day, Victor took care of Alex until he opened the shoe store. For the rest of the day, an elderly woman in an upstairs apartment watched him.

Victor had played baseball in the Dominican Republic, and he passed on his love of the game to his young son. By the time Alex was two years old, he was swinging a red plastic bat and bouncing rubber balls off the walls of the family apartment. The future baseball star sometimes accidentally hit his sister and broke things with his tiny bat and ball. "Alex was a gift," his father says. "Such a good boy. He was always crazy for baseball. He could not get enough."[6] The toddler's initial attempts at baseball were indoors; he had to play inside because it was not safe to play outside in the poor neighborhood the family lived in.

When Alex was four years old, the Rodriguezes returned to the Dominican Republic because they had made enough money to live comfortably in their homeland. It was there that their youngest son began to play the game that would help him achieve fame and fortune.

Learns Baseball

The Dominican Republic is a Spanish-speaking nation that shares the Caribbean island of Hispaniola with Haiti. In 1979 the Rodriguez family moved to Santo Domingo, the nation's capital. They lived in a nice four-bedroom home and had enough money to hire a maid. Alex began attending school and playing baseball, a sport that was even more popular there than in the United States.

Rodriguez has fond memories of learning the game in the Dominican Republic despite a lack of equipment and coping with playing fields that sometimes lacked grass or were very bumpy.

Kids in Santo Domingo gather for a baseball game. Alex Rodriguez's family moved to Santo Domingo in 1979, and Alex began playing baseball there.

"Playing ball was tougher [in the Dominican Republic]," he says. "No one had anything. In the U.S. there were $200 gloves, and the fields were like paradise."[7] Because many children could not buy gloves or balls, they had to play games in which they used sticks to hit kidney beans other kids threw at them. That game is similar to stickball, a game that children in poor U.S. cities play using broom handles to hit tennis or rubber balls while playing in the street.

Alex's father and older brother, Joe, taught Alex the basics of baseball. When Alex was six years old and began playing organized baseball, he hit his first home run, a ball that flew over the head of the third baseman and far into the outfield. He recalls, "I was almost crying, I was so happy."[8] Alex loved the game so much and practiced so hard that his father predicted his son would one day be a star in the major leagues. That did not seem like an impossible dream for someone from the Dominican Republic—players from the Caribbean island like Juan Marichal and Sammy Sosa had become rich and famous playing Major League Baseball.

The Rodriguezes moved back to the United States when Alex was eight years old. The family was having financial problems—the shoe store Victor still owned in New York and a pharmacy in the Dominican Republic he had invested in were not making any money—and his two older children wanted to go to college in the United States. The family relocated to Miami, Florida, where Alex would blossom as a player.

Victor Abandons the Family

Because it was more expensive to live in the United States than in the Dominican Republic, Alex's family could only afford to live in a small apartment in Kendall, a Miami suburb. Alex attended Everglades Elementary School, and the fourth grader struggled with his studies because he spoke little English. In both New York and the Dominican Republic, Alex's family had spoken Spanish at home, and it took Alex several years to become fluent in English.

A year after the move to Miami, Victor left the family and went to New York. He claimed that he would be able to make more money for his family in New York. Alex was devastated by the absence of his father, whom he loved deeply, and for awhile he believed that Victor would return. "At the time," Rodriguez told a reporter years later, "I was naive enough to think that [his father] didn't like Miami and would eventually come back."[9] But Victor had lied to his son: He actually abandoned his family because he was bored in Miami. Victor and Lourdes soon divorced, which devastated Alex.

Lourdes struggled to support the family, because Victor only occasionally sent money. She worked as a secretary during the day and as a waitress at night. Alex's two older siblings also worked to support the family even though they were still going to school. Lourdes became the focus of the young boy's life. He says, "All the love I had for him [his father] I just gave to my mother. She deserved it."[10]

Just as his mother became more important to him, so did sports, which gave him a release from the feelings of hurt and despair he felt over the loss of his father.

The Young Star

One day when Alex was watching a team play baseball near his elementary school, the team's coach, Juan Diego Arteaga, noticed him and asked if he had ever played catcher. Alex never had, but his father had been a catcher. He wanted to play so much that he lied and said he could play that difficult position. At eight years old, Alex was two years younger than the other kids, but he played well and became a part of the team. He also became best friends with Arteaga's son, Juan Diego, who was nicknamed J.D.

From then on, baseball consumed his life. In addition to Arteaga's team, Alex also played on a Boys & Girls Club team coached by Eddie Rodriguez (who is not related to Alex). Both coaches became father figures to Alex. Eddie, a former minor league player, was already famous for coaching local Latin American youths like Jose Canseco and Danny Tartabull who had made it to the major leagues. He helped the Rodriguez family pay the thirty-two-dollar

Rodriguez joined a baseball team near his elementary school as well as a team for the Boys & Girls Club. Even at age 10, Rodriguez was a great athlete.

fee so Alex could play league baseball. "Because of people like Eddie Rodriguez, I was able to afford that,"[11] Rodriguez recalls. Eddie was glad to help Alex because he was so talented. He says,

> At 10 or 11, you could see he was a great athlete. He could fly [run fast] and he was excellent in any sport he tried. We've had a lot of major-league players come through here but [nobody] has worked harder than Alex. It was a pleasure to have him there. From the day he walked in here when he was nine years old, he was an excellent kid.[12]

The talent Eddie saw in Alex showed itself right away as he won a batting title in his first season playing for the Boys & Girls Club. But even though Alex was starring in games, his mom and siblings rarely saw him play because they worked so much.

A Phenomenal Athlete

Alex Rodriguez was a gifted athlete in many sports. As a freshman at Christopher Columbus High, he was the basketball team's starting point guard and the first freshman ever to start for the team. Rodriguez also played basketball at Westminster Christian High School and was so good that he received scholarship offers from Florida State University and several other colleges. As Westminster's starting quarterback in football, he broke several school records and was named both his junior and senior years to all-state teams. Doug Mientkiewicz played baseball with Rodriguez at Westminster, and they were also teammates when both played for the New York Yankees. Mientkiewicz believes Rodriguez was talented enough to have played professional basketball and football as well as baseball. And he admits he was always awed by how easy it was for Rodriguez to star in several sports. He says,

> Even in high school, he always did stuff that you were like, "That's just not normal." He'd walk by the weight room and put five pounds of muscle on while getting ready for baseball practice. He'd grab a basketball and go dunk it, then take a football and throw it 60 yards in the air. It was just not normal. It's not supposed to happen. It's not supposed to be that easy.

Doug Mientkiewicz and Bill Eichenberger, "You Don't Know [Alex Rodriguez] Like I Know [Alex Rodriguez]." *Sporting News.* September 15, 2008, p. 70.

Alex was a great all-around athlete who also excelled at football and basketball. In his freshman season at Christopher Columbus High School, he was good enough in basketball to start as a point guard. But baseball was his great passion. Like many youngsters Alex collected baseball cards—he once had two hundred thousand of them—and decorated his room with posters of baseball stars. His favorite player was Baltimore Orioles shortstop Cal Ripken Jr., whom he idolized.

When Alex failed to win a starting position in baseball, he decided to switch to Westminster Christian School, the private school J.D. attended. Westminster had one of the nation's most renowned baseball programs, and it was there that Alex developed into one of the best young players in the country.

A National Championship

Tuition at Westminster was five thousand dollars a year, far more than Alex's family could afford, but Arteaga arranged financial aid so Alex could attend the elite sports school. Since Westminster was a long way from his home, Alex had to leave at 6:30 A.M. to get to school, and he did not return until 8 P.M. or later because of classes and after-school practice in the sports he played year-round. Alex's mom gave him twenty dollars a day to buy his meals. As an adult, Rodriguez would realize how much his mother sacrificed to give him that much money every day.

Alex excelled at several sports at Westminster. But during his sophomore football season, Alex had one of the most horrible experiences of his life. Arteaga, who was in the stands to watch Alex and his son play, became ill during halftime. He died after being taken to the hospital, and his death was hard on Alex. "He was the guy who treated me like his third child," Rodriguez says. "He just had a stroke and passed away. So that was a tough time."[13]

When Alex entered Westminster as a sophomore, he was 6-feet, 1-inch tall and weighed only 155 pounds (70kg). After a so-so sophomore season in which he hit a batting average of .256, Alex dedicated himself to improving. One way was to lift weights to get stronger, and when he returned as a junior, he had gained 25 pounds (11kg). Rich Hofman, his high school baseball coach, said Alex worked harder to get strong than any player he had ever coached. "When we'd get done working out for two or three hours and the others would go home, he would go into the weight room for hours on his own,"[14] Hofman said. Alex also improved by taking advice from Hofman about being a better hitter, learning, for example, to be more selective about which pitches to hit.

While attending Westminster Christian School, Rodriguez played ball on the same team as Doug Mientkiwicz, pictured here, who would later be his teammate on the New York Yankees.

Alex was so strong as a junior that he could hit a ball 400 feet (122m), which allowed him to hit "pool shots"—home runs driven over the fence of the school's baseball field and into an adjacent swimming pool. His strength and new patience at the plate helped him have a breakout season as he batted .477 with

41 runs batted in (RBI) and stole 42 bases to lead Westminster to a 33–2 record and the Florida state championship. Westminster was so good that the National High School Baseball Coaches Association and *Baseball America* magazine both chose it as the nation's top high school team in 1992.

Although Alex was the star, there were other good players on the Westminster team. One of them was Doug Mientkiewicz, a close friend who would later be Rodriguez's teammate on the New York Yankees. Rodriguez often borrowed clothes from Mientkiewicz, whose family was well-off. What Mientkiewicz remembers the most about his friend was how hard he worked to improve his baseball skills. He says, "The one thing about him that I've learned and always appreciated is that no one outworks him at anything. He's been that way since he was 16 years old, since I have known him. He outworks every single athlete on earth."[15]

That effort paid off in Alex's senior year when he became the nation's most talked-about high school player. Alex was so good going into his senior season that he was expected to be the number-one pick in the 1993 baseball draft of amateur players, which would guarantee him a contract worth several million dollars. The teenager loved the attention but claimed that he was not overly concerned about being chosen first. If Alex was not picked—which was unlikely—his backup plan was to attend the University of Miami on a baseball scholarship. "I can't worry whether I will go in the third round or the first round or play at Miami," Alex told one reporter in the spring of 1993. "Whatever happens, happens."[16]

Chapter 2

Becoming a Star

In 1993, the summer before his senior year of high school, Alex Rodriguez was in Monterey, Mexico, playing for the U.S. team in the World Junior Championships. He impressed many major league scouts when he hit 6 home runs and had 16 runs batted in (RBIs). Seattle Mariners scout Fernando Arguelles says, "That's when I first thought, 'This kid's got a chance to be a big-time player. This could be the next Cal Ripken, Jr.' He was a man as a child."[17] Ripken was the perennial all-star shortstop of the Baltimore Orioles and one of the sport's best shortstops. Shortstop was the same position Rodriguez played.

In August that year, Hurricane Andrew carved a wide swath of destruction through southern Florida. The Miami area was hit hard, including Westminster Christian School. The start of Rodriguez's senior year was delayed six weeks so storm damage to Westminster could be repaired. Rodriguez starred again as a quarterback in football but decided not to play basketball because he wanted to prepare himself for the baseball season. He knew that if he had another great season in baseball, he would have a chance to play in the major leagues.

The Number-One Draft Pick

Every June major league teams hold their annual draft of amateur players. To make sure they select the best players available, teams send representatives, known as scouts, to evaluate the nation's best high school and college players. In March 1993 when Rodriguez played the first game of his senior high school

Alex Rodriguez listens on the phone while the Seattle Mariners ask him to join their team.

season, sixty-eight scouts were on hand to record his every move. Usually only one or two scouts turn out to watch a promising young player. The fact that so many scouts showed up was a testament to Rodriguez's talents, which they had learned about from reports about his junior season and from seeing him play during the junior tournament in Mexico.

Scouts valued the 6-foot, 3-inch (1.9m), 195-pound (88kg) shortstop because he was skilled in the "five tools" of baseball—hitting for average, hitting for power, running speed, arm strength, and fielding ability. At the first practice, a reporter asked an American League team-scouting director about Rodriguez, and the scout gushed, "He's the best (amateur prospect) I've ever seen. He's as talented as Ken Griffey Jr., but he plays with more intensity."[18] Comparing Rodriguez to Griffey was high praise because Griffey, an outfielder who had been the first selection of the Seattle Mariners in the 1987 draft, was considered one of baseball's best players.

The Economics of Baseball

Alex Rodriguez quickly learned the harsh nature of baseball economics after the Seattle Mariners drafted him on June 3, 1993. Although Rodriguez wanted to play professional baseball more than he wanted to go to college, he had previously signed a letter of intent to attend the University of Miami. Rodriguez did that because he and his agent, Scott Boras, knew they could use his admission by Miami as a bargaining ploy to get more money from the Mariners. During the nearly two months it took for the Mariners and Rodriguez to agree on a contract, he commented several times that he would be content to play college baseball if the Mariners did not offer him enough money. But as the contract stalemate continued, Rodriguez learned how hard it is to be involved in multimillion-dollar contract talks, and he eventually signed for less money than he had originally demanded.

Rodriguez had another economic lesson that summer when Team USA, which represents the United States in international competition, invited him to try out for the team. It was an honor because Rodriguez was the first high school player asked to try out for the team. Topps, a baseball card company, sponsored Team USA and wanted to issue player cards. But Rodriguez refused to participate because he had already signed a deal with another card company that paid him five hundred thousand dollars for the rights to his first baseball card. Due to the dispute between the card companies, he was denied the honor of playing for Team USA.

The attention from scouts and reporters who flocked to his games amazed the seventeen-year-old Rodriguez. However, he was savvy enough to realize why they were there. He told one reporter for a national magazine, "My mom told me that all the scouts are here because they see something they like."[19] Rodriguez gave everyone even more to like with a fantastic senior season. He hit a batting average of .505 with 9 home runs and 36 RBI and stole 35 bases in 44 games to showcase the unique combination of power and speed that made him a sensational major league prospect.

On June 3, the Mariners chose Rodriguez with the first selection in the draft. Rodriguez's joy at being the top draft pick was marred by a telephone call from his father to congratulate him. "He had no right to be part of it,"[20] Rodriguez said.

The Business of Baseball

Seattle Mariners general manager Woody Woodward told reporters he believed Rodriguez would quickly agree to a contract with the team because the Mariners would offer him fair terms. Rodriguez was not happy about being selected by the Mariners because he wanted to play for a National League team, but he knew that baseball was a business as well as a sport. He hired agent Scott Boras, who was known for getting the most money possible for his clients, to negotiate his contract. To strengthen his bargaining position with the Mariners, Rodriguez accepted a baseball scholarship to the University of Miami. If the Mariners did not sign Rodriguez by the time school started in August, it would lose rights to him, and he could be drafted again the following year.

Boras asked for a $2.5 million contract and a $1 million signing bonus, but the Mariners countered with a $1 million overall offer. Rodriguez stayed out of contract talks, leaving them to Boras, who consulted with family members Lourdes and Suzy Rodriguez.

In the meantime, Team USA, which represents the nation in international competition, had invited him to try out for the squad. He was the first high school player asked to play for Team USA, but after trying out Rodriguez wasn't able to play for the team due to a dispute between two baseball card companies about who owned the rights to sell his card. After that, Rodriguez joined one of the teams in the U.S. Olympic Festival in San Antonio, Texas. While he was at the festival in July, he admitted to a reporter that the extended contract talks with the Mariners were wearing him down. His whole future in playing the game he loved was at stake. He said, "I wish they would just tell me, 'Look, we're not going to sign you.' I'd say, 'O.K., I'm going to college.' It's dragging it out. This is a business decision.

After a long series of negotiations, Rodriguez joined the Seattle Mariners. A few hours later he would have been ineligible because he would have begun classes at the University of Miami.

If they want to pay me what they said all year I'm worth, I'll play; if not I'll go to college."[21]

One day later, an errant pregame throw by another player hit Rodriguez while he was relaxing in the dugout and broke his right cheekbone. Three days after the accident, he underwent plastic surgery to repair the injury, which had created a depression, or dent, in his face. A doctor surgically inserted a rod in his face to force the depressed cheekbone back to its normal shape. Doctors told Rodriguez he could have died if the ball had hit him 1 inch (2.5cm) higher. The injury made Rodriguez and his family worry that another injury could rob him of his opportunity to make a lot of money in baseball. The family even took out an insurance policy that would pay Rodriguez $1 million if that happened.

When Boras continued to seek a bigger bonus than the Mariners wanted to give Rodriguez, his mother and sister began to take a stronger role in the talks. They convinced Rodriguez to accept less money. The deal with the Mariners was not finalized until 3 A.M. on August 30, just hours before Rodriguez was scheduled to attend a psychology class at the University of Miami, which would have officially made him a student and ineligible to sign the pact. The three-year contract was for $1.3 million with a $500,000 signing bonus. At a news conference, Rodriguez expressed his relief that the talks were over so he could begin his professional career.

The Struggling Teenage Player

Because the minor league season had already ended, Rodriguez's introduction to professional baseball was limited that fall to several weeks in an instructional league for young players. In April 1994 Rodriguez was assigned to the Mariner's Class-A team in Appleton, Wisconsin, the lowest of its top-three minor league teams. Professional baseball teams operate minor league teams to help players improve their skills enough so they can play in the major leagues. The teams assess young players and assign them to minor league teams based on their skill level. As players improve, they are promoted to higher levels. The three top levels are Class A, Class AA, and Class AAA, also referred to as Triple A, the highest minor league level. Because he was so young, Rodriguez began his professional career in Class A. Rodriguez admitted he suffered in Wisconsin's frigid spring weather. He says, "It was cold. We had to rake snow off the field. But the people up there were great. I think the people in the Midwest are the friendliest people in the entire country."[22]

Rodriguez played so well that he was not cold for very long. After hitting .379 with 14 home runs and 55 RBI in only 65 games, Rodriguez was promoted to Class AA in Jacksonville, Florida, where he smashed a home run in his first at bat. After hitting .391 in 17 games there, he played briefly for Seattle's Triple-A affiliate team, the Calgary Cannons. Then, the eighteen-year-old was called up to the Mariners on July 7, 1994. He made his major league debut in Boston, Massachusetts, the next day against the Red Sox, just thirteen months after graduating from high school. At eighteen years, eleven months, Rodriguez was the youngest

The Mariners' Two Young Stars

When two stars play for one team, they sometimes have trouble getting along because each resents any attention the other gets. But when Alex Rodriguez began playing well enough in 1996 to rival Ken Griffey Jr., who had been the Mariners' biggest star for several seasons, the two players remained friendly. In interviews Rodriguez acknowledged Griffey's status as the team's leader and best player while Griffey expressed his joy that the Mariners had another power hitter to help the club win. The two became friends when Rodriguez went to Seattle after signing his contract, and Griffey later helped

Ken Griffey Jr. was on the Mariners with Rodriguez.

Rodriguez adapt to major league life. In a newspaper story in August 1996, their good relationship was apparent when they playfully talked to reporter Selena Roberts about how Rodriguez had been using Griffey's bats. Roberts writes,

> So far this season, Rodriguez has delivered 28 home runs and 96 runs batted in. What's his secret? "He's using my bats," a smiling Griffey said after the game. Griffey wasn't kidding, either. Rodriguez had gone through all of his [own] bats—broke and cracked each one—when he asked Griffey to borrow one of his. "My bats are in. And they're the same as his. But I've been using his bats for two and a half months," Rodriguez said. "He's probably mad at me, but I'll keep using them until I hit a slump."

Selena Roberts, "Rodriguez, a New Yorker, at Home in Seattle," *New York Times*, August 18, 1996.

Rodriguez quickly joined the major leagues, thirteen months after high school graduation, when he played for the Mariners against the Red Sox.

player to debut in the major leagues since 1984. "It's funny," he said. "Last year I would have paid anything to go watch a major league game. This year I'm playing in one."[23] On July 9 Rodriguez got his first major league hit, a single.

It was unusual for any player to rise through the minor leagues so fast, especially for a teenager. Although the Mariners had planned to call him up in September when teams could have more players on their roster, Manager Lou Piniella was anxious to see if he was ready for the major leagues. Rodriguez was a good infielder but struggled at the plate, hitting .204 in 17 games before the Mariners sent him back down to Calgary on August 2. Rodriguez's low batting average of .204—an infielder should hit at least .250 to be considered respectable—indicated he needed more minor league experience and instruction to handle major league pitching.

When the season ended, Rodriguez realized he needed to improve, so he played in the Dominican Republic's winter league. Many major league players have done that to sharpen their skills because the games are very competitive. "It was the toughest experience of my life," says Rodriguez. "I just got my tail kicked and learned how hard this game can be. It was brutal, but I recommend it to every young player."[24] Rodriguez batted only .179, and he admitted the experience made him realize how hard he had to work to be ready for the major leagues.

The 1995 season was disappointing for Rodriguez. He was shuttled back and forth between the Mariners and its Triple-A team in Tacoma, Washington, because Luis Sojo and Felix Fermin were performing better at shortstop for the Mariners than he was. In August, when Rodriguez was sent back down to Triple A for the third time, he said, "I understand the move and I'm not mad about it, but four or five times a year gets old. I don't consider this a setback, but I hope these bumps in the road are eliminated real soon."[25] Rodriguez was so demoralized that he considered quitting baseball, but his mother talked him out of it.

Rodriguez ended the season positively when he was recalled to the Mariners on August 31. When the team won the American League West Division title, he was excited to play in two postseason games, even though he failed to get a hit. The Mariners beat the New York Yankees in the Division Series before losing to the Cleveland Indians in the American League Championship Series to end their season. The playoff experience thrilled him so much that he told reporters, "It's kind of ironic, isn't it? At first, I didn't want to play [with the Mariners]. Now I can't imagine playing anywhere else. This is the perfect place for me."[26]

His Breakout Season

In 1995 Rodriguez hit only .232 in 48 games with the Mariners. But in spring training in 1996 Piniella decided to make the talented twenty-year-old his starting shortstop because he believed Rodriguez had learned a lot about the pressure of playing while the team battled for a division title. "Quite frankly," Piniella says, "Alex was ready."[27] Rodriguez justified Piniella's faith in him during the 1996 season opener by hitting a game-winning single in the twelfth inning to drive in the winning run in a 3–2 victory over the Chicago White Sox. The game on March 31 was the first season opener in March, and Rodriguez's first opening day start. It also marked the beginning of a season in which he would shine as one of the game's brightest young stars.

To the delight of Mariners fans, Rodriguez had one of the best seasons any young shortstop ever had. In 146 games he batted .358 to lead hitters in both the American and National Leagues.

When Rodriguez played backup to shortstop Cal Ripkin Jr. during an All-Star Game, he got to meet and play ball with one of his childhood idols.

It was also the highest batting average of any player who began the season younger than twenty-one since Ty Cobb, who hit .350 in 1907. Rodriguez's 215 hits were also the most by a shortstop in one season, and he smashed 36 home runs and drove in 123 RBI, huge power numbers for an infielder.

Rodriguez played so well that he was chosen for the All-Star Game as a backup to shortstop Cal Ripken Jr. Being an all-star is

The New Media Star

The news media did hundreds of stories about Alex Rodriguez during the 1996 season when he blossomed into one of the best players in baseball. Gerry Callahan of *Sports Illustrated* magazine was one of many reporters who described Rodriguez's sterling character as well as his vast on-field abilities. In July 1996 he wrote,

> Most people don't yet know what kind of person Rodriguez is, but they are quickly learning that as a ball-player he's almost too good to be true. He is 6'3" and 195 pounds of pure skill and grace, an immensely gifted shortstop who [can] run, hit, hit for power and make all the plays in the field. He's the youngest position player in the American League, but already he has turned his potential into performance. "He's the type of kid you build an organization around," says Seattle right-fielder Jay Buhner. [He] appears to be as flawless as a hot fudge sundae, so finally you ask one of his Mariners team-mates if Rodriguez is on the level. Is he really this polite, this smart, this sweet, or am I being played like another Nintendo game? "Well, he's definitely a good kid," says the teammate. "But you know all that stuff like, 'Oh, gee, I'm just happy to be in the big leagues?' Well, that's an act. Don't let him fool you. He knows how good he is. And he knows how good he's going to be."

Gerry Callahan, "The Fairest of Them All." *Sports Illustrated*, July 8, 1996, p. 38.

a huge honor. But for Rodriguez, the biggest thrill was meeting Ripken, his childhood idol. During practice the day before the game, Ripken walked up to him and said, "Hi, my name is Cal Ripken Jr., I couldn't wait to meet you. I've heard so much about you."[28] It was a memorable moment for Rodriguez as well as a sign that he had arrived as a player.

By August Rodriguez was taking for granted his almost super-human achievements. In a game in New York against the Yankees, he became only the tenth player since Yankee Stadium had been renovated in 1975 to hit a home run far enough to reach the black background beyond the center-field wall. "I didn't even watch it," Rodriguez said nonchalantly of the 416-foot (127m) blast. "I knew I hit it well, but I didn't know where it landed. I didn't know there was history behind it."[29] Such exploits earned him *Sporting News* magazine's Major League Player of the Year award and the Associated Press Player of the Year honors. He was a candidate for the Most Valuable Player award, which is given every year by the Baseball Writers Association of America, but lost to Juan Gonzalez of the Texas Rangers.

The Mariners were so impressed with his play that in July they gave him a four-year contract extension worth $10.5 million. Just hours after Rodriguez signed it, he smashed his twenty-seventh home run in a 13–7 win over the Detroit Tigers, proving he was worth the expensive contract. Making a lot of money, however, did not seem to change him very much, at least, not right away.

The Life of a Star

When Rodriguez signed his rookie contract with the Mariners, he went from being poor to being rich. His lifestyle, however, did not alter dramatically. His one big expenditure was to buy a $34,000 Jeep Cherokee. Rodriguez then limited himself to a $1,000 per month allowance, a small sum for someone making as much money as he was. He did use some of his wealth to help his mom and siblings, and in the off-season he lived with his mom, sharing a bedroom with Ripper, his three-year-old German shepherd.

Though Rodriguez quickly gained wealth with his first professional baseball contract, he gave himself an allowance, helped his family, and gave to charity.

The news media liked Rodriguez, who was always polite and said nice things about other players. Shortly before he turned twenty-one on July 27, 1996, a reporter asked Rodriguez if he liked beer. He amazed the reporter by saying he could not stand how it tasted. He also told the reporter why he tried to be a good person. He said, "My mom always said, 'I don't care if you turn out to be a terrible ballplayer, I just want you to be a good person'. That's the most important thing to me. Like Cal [Ripken, Jr.] or Dale Murphy [his childhood baseball heroes], I want people to look at me and say, 'He's a good person.'"[30]

One way Rodriguez carried out this goal was by being charitable. After the 1996 season, he gave $25,000 to a Miami unit of the Boys & Girls Clubs of America, so it could build a new baseball field. It was his way of giving back to an organization that had helped him fulfill his dream of playing Major League Baseball.

Chapter 3

The Best Player in Baseball

During the 1997 season, Alex Rodriguez had a batting average of .300 with 23 home runs and 84 runs batted in (RBI) for the Seattle Mariners. Those are superb statistics for a shortstop. But because they paled in comparison to the sensational numbers Rodriguez had achieved one year earlier, some people wondered if his fantastic season had been a fluke. In the next three years, Rodriguez proved those doubters wrong and solidified his reputation as one of baseball's best players by smashing at least 40 home runs and driving in at least 100 RBI each season. In 1998 Rodriguez also joined one of baseball's most elite clubs, the 40–40 club, when he hit 42 home runs and stole 46 bases. He was just the third player in major league history to earn 40 or more home runs and 40 or more stolen bases in a season. The twenty-two-year-old Rodriguez was the youngest to do it—Jose Canseco was one year older in 1988 and nine years younger than Barry Bonds when he accomplished the difficult feat in 1996.

The combination of so much raw home-run power and base-stealing speed made Rodriguez one of baseball's finest players. And because his defensive skills as shortstop, one of the game's most difficult positions, were higher than those of Canseco or Bonds, who were rather ordinary outfielders, some people considered Rodriguez the best player in baseball. One of these admirers was teammate David Segui, who after Rodriguez hit his fortieth homer on September 19, 1998, gave him a bottle of champagne with the message "Congrats on 40/40" taped to it. Segui says,

Rodriguez sliding into base after stealing second. A-Rod became the third "40–40" player in major league history when he hit 42 home runs and stole 46 bases.

"He's the best ballplayer in the game. Definitely, [Barry] Bonds and [Ken Griffey] Junior are up there with him, but the way he plays the game sets him apart from everyone else, I think. [He] plays the game the way it's supposed to be played, plays to win. I'm not alone in [saying] this: He's the best in the game."[31]

The question of who is the best player in any sport can be endlessly debated. However, many people agreed with Segui, a talented player who played professionally from 1990 to 2004, because Rodriguez had been playing at a very high level for so long. Rodriguez had also continued to make history—his forty-two home runs in 1998 were a season record for American League shortstops—while being selected annually for the All-Star Team.

Rodriguez's natural athletic talent was a major factor in his sensational play. Mariners batting coach Lee Elia, who coached great hitters like Mike Schmidt, Don Mattingly, and Ryne Sandberg, said in 1999 that Rodriguez was as good or better than all of them. "With his ability," Elia said, "there's no telling what he can accomplish."[32] Ability, though, was only one factor. Rodriguez's work ethic, which compelled him to keep improving, was also responsible for his becoming a great player.

Rodriguez Works Hard

One of the keys to Rodriguez's success in the 1996 season was that he had studied hard during the off-season to become a better hitter. For the second straight year, the young player set aside three days a week to watch three-hours' worth of tapes of teammate Edgar Martinez, a great hitter who batted .312 in eighteen seasons with the Mariners. The tapes had all of Martinez's hits from 1994 and 1995. Rodriguez believed he could learn from watching how a great hitter handled different pitchers and the pitches they threw. Rodriguez did not limit his knowledge seeking to teammates. He was even willing to seek

Pushing to be Better

Coaches and players agree that one of Alex Rodriguez's biggest assets is that he works hard to get better. In a 1999 magazine article titled "Aiming To Be the Best" former Mariners teammate David Segui explains what impressed him the most about Rodriguez:

> There's nothing he doesn't do extraordinarily well. He plays hard every day. People say, "You're making millions of dollars a year, you should play hard every day." Some days your body just doesn't go, no matter how hard you tell it to go. No matter how much money you're making, you're still a human being, and your body only functions to certain levels. Alex works extra, he prepares himself. He does a lot of little things that kids his age haven't begun to think about. Most kids his age show up and assume that they're going to be here 10 years, that they have plenty of time, and that there's no urgency in getting better. They play on their natural ability. He takes the few extra steps to get better—that's what's impressive.

Quoted in John Lowe, "Aiming To Be the Best," *Baseball Digest*, October 1999, p. 46.

help from rival players like Rickey Henderson, the all-time career leader in stolen bases with 1,406. When the Mariners played Henderson's Oakland A's, Rodriguez discussed base-stealing tactics with him.

Rodriguez also worked hard during spring training in 1996 to adjust to the major league strike zone, which is smaller than that in college baseball, to avoid striking out. Manager Lou Piniella said that as the weeks went by he saw Rodriguez improve at discerning balls from strikes. Rodriguez also worked with Elia to make mechanical adjustments in his swing that helped him retain his power while giving him more control of the bat. Elia explains,

Seeking to become a better ball player, Rodriguez sought advice from others, including rivals like Rickey Henderson.

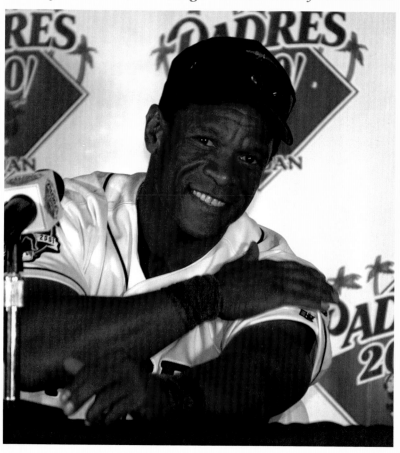

"We worked [to shorten] up on it, making him understand that he had enough leverage and enough bat speed through the hitting area that he didn't have to stay long."[33]

After his disappointing 1997 season, Rodriguez realized that he had to do even more to become a great player. He hired a personal trainer and worked out five to six times a week in the off-season to improve his strength and conditioning. Rodriguez also continued to study videos to learn more about hitting. Rodriguez explained how his 1997 swoon forced him to rededicate himself, and it helped him become a "40–40" player in 1998:

> It's just a great lesson for me as a young player about the necessity of hard work. That's what I attribute my success to last season, all my work. It's probably the thing I'm most proud of, more than being the batting champion (in 1996). This is something I'm very, very proud of and something I'll never forget.[34]

Rodriguez's disciplined approach to working hard at learning the game and keeping himself in shape helped him become one of baseball's greatest hitters from 1998 through 2000. The fame and fortune that came with those accomplishments changed Rodriguez's life in many ways, from living in luxurious homes to being recognized wherever he went.

A Star's Lifestyle

For several years of his early baseball career, Rodriguez rented a large apartment in downtown Seattle, Washington, but in 2000 he moved to a house on Mercer Island so his three dogs would have more room to run around. Rodriguez still spent his off-seasons in Miami, but in a home he owned instead of at his mother's house. By 2001 Rodriguez had enough money to travel to the Dominican Republic to play golf, and he often took along friends and family members. He also went fishing on *Sweet Swing*, a luxury boat that could sleep six people and had three televisions. It was a $600,000 boat, but Rodriguez liked to brag, "I bought it for $270,000. I'm a bargain guy."[35]

Rodriguez was noted by People *magazine as being one of the best-dressed athletes, often appearing in suits and ties. He maintained a clean image and a down-to-earth attitude.*

Rodriguez surprised a lot of people during the 1998 off-season by taking classes in writing and political science at Miami-Dade Community College. The twenty-two-year-old enjoyed going to school, especially his writing class. He says, "[Writing is] a great skill to have, and I need to work on mine. You want to be able to write a thank-you note or letters or whatever. It's a skill I want to have."[36] It did not take long for his classmates to realize they had a celebrity in their midst. When they did, Rodriguez graciously signed the posters and baseball cards they brought to class.

The college courses were Rodriguez's attempt to live up to the way he thought sports stars should conduct themselves. In 1998 he told *People* magazine, "A major league baseball player is no longer solely identified by hitting home runs. You have to speak

Signing Autographs

For many professional athletes signing autographs is part of their job, and it can become a burden because they have to do it so often. But Alex Rodriguez has always been gracious about signing autographs. He told reporter John Hickey in 2000 that he tries to sign his autograph correctly because he knows it means so much to fans who ask for it. Hickey writes,

> [Alex Rodriguez] sat in the Mariners clubhouse signing a few baseballs brought to him by coach John Moses. Generally, players sign balls with a lick and a promise. One signature looks pretty much like another, and some are not all that legible. Not so for Rodriguez. His signatures were all crisp and clear. "I've always tried to do it neatly, because I've been on the other side," Rodriguez said as he sat in front of his locker, signing. "I still remember my favorite autograph. One year, Keith Hernandez [a New York Yankee] came down to Miami.... He was working out at Florida International (University). Me and some of my buddies went over there to see if we could get his autograph. We were in the stands about an hour, when he was done with his workout, he waved us into the dugout. I remember that day vividly. It was such a big thrill."

John Hickey, "Mariners' Shortstop Alex Rodriguez Not a Typical Superstar," *Baseball Digest*, July 2000, p. 40.

well, behave well and dress well."[37] His comment appeared in the article, "The 50 Most Beautiful People in the World 1998," in which Rodriguez was one of the fifty. The same article notes that Rodriguez was one of the best-dressed athletes—he owned 60 suits, 65 pairs of dress shoes, 100 shirts, and 250 ties—and was meticulous about maintaining his good looks. He washed his face with Clinique soap, had a haircut every ten days, had a manicure and pedicure once a month, and flossed his teeth four times a day.

The well-groomed star was on display not only in magazines like *People* and *GQ*—Rodriguez and fellow shortstops Derek Jeter and Nomar Garciaparra were on the magazine's cover in April 2000—but also in television ads for products like Speed Stick deodorant. His face and form even made their way into computer games like Triple Play 99. A lot of athletes get conceited from that much attention, but according to Segui, Rodriguez remained a good person. He says, "He's Mr. Clean. He's milk and cookies. He doesn't like to hear that, but he is. He likes everybody in here [the Mariners clubhouse] to think he's some kind of thug from Miami, but he's as milk-and-cookies as it gets. He's a good guy."[38]

Like many sports stars, Rodriguez received a lot of attention from women. He received thousands of letters from female fans. Mariners catcher John Marzano, a close friend, admitted in 1998 that "everywhere we go, women go nuts."[39] By 1998, however, Rodriguez was steadily dating Cynthia Scurtis, a Miami high school psychology teacher he met in 1996 while both were working out at a gym in Florida. They began dating even though Rodriguez spent half of the year in Seattle. Scurtis declined his invitation to quit her job and live with him in Seattle. She told a reporter she did not worry about Rodriguez when he was away. She recalled, "People are always telling me, 'Oh, he's 23, he's so good-looking, he has all this money. How can you trust him?' But all you have to do is know him. That's all."[40]

Even though baseball separated them, Scurtis could hardly begrudge Rodriguez his passion for the game. When Rodriguez was playing, he did everything he could to help the Mariners be successful. But even the great seasons Rodriguez had were not enough to help the Mariners win a world championship.

Failing to Win a Championship

From 1997 to 2000 A-Rod continued to excel as an individual player and to break records. On June 6, 1997, he became the first Mariners player to hit for the cycle—a single, a double, a triple, and a home run in the same game—during a 14-6 victory over the Detroit Tigers. A month later on July 8, Rodriguez became

San Francisco Giants pitcher Orel Hershiser hit Rodriguez when he was at bat during a game on June 14, 1998. It was just one event in a season of difficulties for the Mariners, who failed to take a championship that year.

the only other shortstop besides Cal Ripken Jr. to start an All-Star Game since 1983. And on July 30, 1999, he hit his first home run at Kauffman Stadium in Kansas City to become one of the few players to homer in every American League ballpark. Some of Rodriguez's individual feats amazed people and added to his growing reputation as a great ball player. For example, after missing thirty-two games during the 1999 season because of a knee injury, Rodriguez hit a home run in his first at bat when he returned to action. Because many players struggle after being sidelined that long, it was considered a remarkable feat.

Rodriguez is also known for his steady on-field attitude. For example, many players become angry if a pitch hits them. Rodriguez ignores beanballs, even if they are intentional, like the one on June 14, 1998, when San Francisco Giants pitcher Orel Hershiser deliberately hit him. Instead of yelling or charging the pitcher's mound, Rodriguez calmly walked to first base, the consolation for being hit. Afterward he said, "It's all a part of the game" and claimed "it didn't hurt."[41] Rodriguez took it calmly because he knew the pitch was in retaliation for his aggressive slide a day earlier that had injured Giants second baseman Jeff Kent.

The Mariners had only one losing season from 1996 to 2000—in 1999 when Rodriguez missed a lot of games with his injury and the team finished 79–83—but they only made the playoffs in 1997 and 2000 and never advanced to the World Series. That seemed to be a poor showing for a team that also had hard-hitting stars like Edgar Martinez and Ken Griffey Jr. As a result, fans and the news media began to criticize the team for not having accomplished more.

The player targeted the most for the mediocre showing was Ken Griffey Jr., because he had been the team's acknowledged leader for several years. The criticism angered him and soured his relationship with Rodriguez, whom he believed should have also been blamed for not winning a championship. During this period, Griffey also became jealous of A-Rod's growing fame. When the Mariners gave away T-shirts honoring Rodriguez, Griffey complained that the club had never done the same for him. Baseball historian Mark Ribowsky claims that by 1999 "[Griffey's] uneasy alliance with Alex Rodriguez had turned paranoid as he feared that A-Rod was usurping his grip on the team and the town."[42]

Griffey's growing unease with the Mariners led him to seek a trade. In February 2000 the Mariners sent the most popular player in team history to the Cincinnati Reds in exchange for four players. The move meant that Rodriguez was now the team's undisputed leader and biggest star.

The 2000 Season

Rodriguez had another outstanding season in 2000 with a .316 average, 41 home runs, and 132 RBI to lead the Mariners into the playoffs. He helped the team beat the Chicago White Sox in the first round, and they then played the New York Yankees

In the 2000 season, the Mariners faced off against the Yankees in the playoffs. Rodriguez led his team well, but they lost to the Yankees, who went on to win the World Series.

for the American League Championship and the right to advance to the World Series against the National League champion. The Yankees had won the 1999 World Series and were favored to repeat as champions. When the Yankees won two of the first three games in the seven game series, the Mariners badly needed a victory in game four.

The Yankees won game four 5–0, and one of the key at bats came in the first inning when Rodriguez came to the plate with

Alex Rodriguez and Cynthia Scurtis

Alex Rodriguez was attracted to Cynthia Scurtis during the off-season in 1996 when he saw her at a gym in Miami. He talked to her several times while they worked out. At first she was not interested in him, even though she knew he was a professional baseball player. But after Rodriguez kept asking for a date, Scurtis finally gave him her telephone number. They dated for six years before marrying in 2002. One of the reasons Scurtis liked Rodriguez was that he seemed to have a mature outlook on life. In an interview in 1999 Scurtis explained,

> He understands that he's 23 going on 24 and he understands that things are going to change. He doesn't want or need to have everything right now. He doesn't do things on impulse. He thinks them through. But it's such a quick process with him. He doesn't open his mouth without thinking things through, but he thinks things through so fast, it just flows. It's a natural gift. [He] can be acting foolish, like a kid, one minute. And the next minute, if you ask him a serious question, he just switches over and he's like a 45-year-old man who's had a million life experiences.

Quoted in Michael Knisley, "All-A-Rod, All the Time," *Sporting News*, June 28, 1999, p. 12.

two outs. Pitching for the Yankees was Roger Clemens, one of the greatest pitchers in the history of baseball. Determined to dominate A-Rod, Clemens fired a ball toward his head that made Rodriguez fall over backward to avoid getting hit. His next pitch was another inside fastball nearly as close to his head. Clemens walked Rodriguez because of the two message pitches, but many people believe the throws set the tone that allowed Clemens to dominate the Mariners line-up for a victory. Even Mariners catcher Joe Oliver says, "Clemens essentially beat the Mariners when he threw those two inside pitches to Rodriguez."[43] The Yankees went on to win the championship in six games even though Rodriguez batted .409 with a 2 home runs and 5 RBI in the series. The Yankees then beat the New York Mets in the World Series.

Rodriguez was named the Major League Player of the Year by the *Baseball America* magazine and finished third for the American League's Most Valuable Player award. He showed in 2000 that he could lead the Mariners to greatness but there was doubt at the end of the season that he would continue with the team because his contract was up. Rodriguez decided to become a free agent, which meant that he could sign with any team in baseball. His decision touched off the biggest bidding war for one player that baseball had ever seen.

Chapter 4

The Nation's Highest-Paid Athlete

Alex Rodriguez drew more media attention during the 2000 season than ever before. Although he had a great year, the flood of stories in newspapers and magazines and on television and radio broadcasts was not confined to how he was playing. Much of the coverage focused on where Rodriguez would be playing the next season and how much he might earn. Rodriguez was in the final year of the 1996 contract he had signed with the Seattle Mariners; when the season ended, he would be a free agent who could sign with any team. Because he was such a great player and only twenty-five years old, the media speculated that some team might offer him one of the richest contracts in sports history. In the December 2000 issue of *Baseball Digest*, baseball writer Mel Antonen made a startling prediction about how much Rodriguez might be worth. He writes,

> It's rare that a player with such youth and skill will be on the open market. Rodriguez already has won a batting championship and is one of three players with 40 home runs and 40 steals in the same season. Last season he hit .316 with 41 home runs, 132 RBI and 134 runs—numbers that warranted Most Valuable Player consideration. Rodriguez could become the first $20 million-a-year player.[44]

To most people, the idea that a player was worth $20 million per season seemed fantasy rather than reality. But just a few weeks after the article appeared in print, Rodriguez signed a blockbuster contract that made sports history.

A Big Payday

Rodriguez was the most highly anticipated free agent since 1975, when baseball players first won the right to move to other teams after their contracts expired. According to Rudy Terasas, a scout for the Texas Rangers, Rodriguez was worth a lot of money

Rodriguez agreed to a ten-year contract with the Texas Rangers for an unprecedented amount of $252 million.

Baseball Free Agents

Alex Rodriguez was able to sign his historic $252-million contract with the Texas Rangers because he was a free agent, which meant he had the right to bargain with any team that wanted to hire him. Baseball players had only been allowed to be free agents for twenty-five years before Rodriguez had his big payday. For decades before that, the "reserve clause" in player contracts bound a player to one team for his entire playing career unless the club decided to trade him. In 1969 Curt Flood, one of baseball's best players, challenged the clause when the St. Louis Cardinals traded him to the Philadelphia Phillies. Flood claimed the trade violated his constitutional rights because the reserve clause made him, a human being, a piece of property that could be owned by a business. He lost his bid to become a free agent who could negotiate with any team when the U.S. Supreme Court ruled in favor of Major League Baseball. But just three years later pitchers Dave Messersmith and Dave McNally also challenged the reserve clause. This time the challenge was handled by Peter Seitz, an independent arbitrator, and in 1975 he ruled the reserve clause only entitled a team to one year of service beyond the expiration of any current contract. The ruling was a boon to players. When they won the right to become free agents, many were able to negotiate bigger salaries from other teams who wanted them.

because he was so good that he could improve any team that signed him. Terasas said, "He's already a complete player. He can beat you in all facets of the game—with his power, his speed, and his glove. [If] I had to take one [player], I'd take A-rod."[45] That was why so many teams, including the Atlanta Braves, New York Mets, New York Yankees, Boston Red Sox, and Seattle Mariners, were interested in Rodriguez.

Scott Boras, A-Rod's agent, realized how valuable Rodriguez was and did his best to get as much money as possible for his client. One tactic he employed was to print one hundred copies of a seventy-three-page book that featured charts and graphs of Rodriguez's career statistics to illustrate that he was already one of the greatest players in baseball history. Boras gave the books, which cost thirty-five thousand dollars to print, to baseball general managers at their annual meeting in Florida in November. When the teams learned Boras thought Rodriguez should be paid $20 million a year, most dropped out of the competition for him because they could not afford such a high salary.

The Seattle Mariners reportedly offered Rodriguez a five-year contract worth $85 million, which he rejected as too low, and the Atlanta Braves wanted Rodriguez but never made an offer. Then the Texas Rangers suddenly became Rodriguez's strongest suitor. The Rangers had won the American League West Division title four times in the 1990s but in 2000 had finished in last place. Owner Tom Hicks, who acquired the team in 1998 from a group that included future president George W. Bush, wanted to win so badly that he decided he wanted Rodriguez no matter how much it cost.

On December 11, Hicks announced that Rodriguez had agreed to a ten-year contract worth $252 million. Hicks explained that he was willing to pay that much because "I like to win. This gives us a chance to leapfrog [to a level of play] people never thought we could get to."[46] Although the Rangers' big acquisition would fail to accomplish that, the unprecedented contract would send salaries soaring in baseball as well as every other professional sport.

The Burden of Big Money

The size of Rodriguez's contract with the Rangers was so immense that it shocked people. The contract was for $2 million more than Hicks had paid two years earlier for the Rangers Ballpark in Arlington, Texas, and the 270 acres surrounding the stadium. Rodriguez's yearly salary under the contract also seemed fantastic. In a year in which the average U.S. worker earned only $28,000 annually, the Rangers agreed to give Rodriguez a $10 million

The contract Rodriguez signed with the Texas Rangers was $2 million more than the team's owner had paid for The Ballpark in Arlington, Texas, where the team played.

signing bonus and annual salaries of between $21 and $27 million over the course of the contract.

In addition to being critical of how much money Rodriguez would get, many people also expressed fears that his historic deal would hurt baseball. Sandy Alderson, Major League Baseball's vice president of baseball operations, said, "To me it's incredible. We clearly have a crisis situation in the game. It's time for us to deal with it. This contract will affect every team's ability to operate in the system."[47] Baseball Commissioner Allan "Bud" Selig and many other people believed the contract would result in much bigger salaries for other star players. When that happened, they claimed, only rich teams in big cities like New York would be able to sign enough star players to win a championship. That prediction already seemed to be coming true. Even though Rodriguez's contract was the biggest, two free agent pitchers also received huge new contracts. The Yankees signed pitcher Mike Mussina for six years and $88.5 million while the Colorado Rockies got pitcher Mike Hampton for eight years and $121 million.

Rodriguez's contract was also attacked because it seemed ridiculous to give so much money to just one player in a sport in which all twenty-five players on a team needed to contribute to ensure a good season. Lawrence Hadley, an associate professor of economics at the University of Dayton in Ohio, says, "You can't build a team around one star player in baseball. You might be able to do that in basketball [whose teams have fewer players], but not in baseball."[48] A single star basketball player like Michael Jordan can dominate enough during games to help his team win championships, but in baseball it is harder for one player to ensure such success.

A Historic and Giant Contract

When Alex Rodriguez signed a ten-year, $252-million contract with the Texas Rangers in 2000, the amount of money shocked people. It was twice the total value and average annual salary of the previous biggest contract for a U.S. athlete in any sport—the six-year, $126-million contract that basketball star Kevin Garnett had signed with the Minnesota Timberwolves in 1997. One reason the contract seemed extravagant was that it was worth more than the estimated value of eighteen major league teams, including the Chicago Cubs at $242 million, San Francisco Giants at $237 million, St. Louis Cardinals at $219 million, and Detroit Tigers at $200 million. It was also $2 million more than Texas owner Tom Hicks had paid just two years earlier for the entire team; its stadium in Arlington, Texas; and the nearly 200 acres (81ha) of land surrounding the stadium .

The contract was for so much money that reporters had fun trying to put it into perspective by figuring out how much Rodriguez would have earned in 2000 for his statistics in various hitting categories. Based on his 2000 numbers, his $21 million salary for 2001 meant that he was paid $170,000 for every game he played, $45,487 for every at bat, $144,000 for every hit, $614,634 for every home run, and $190,909 for every run batted in (RBI).

Rodriguez was ecstatic over his good fortune in getting paid so much money even though he seemed stunned that the Rangers had signed him. "People hadn't talked about Texas, so I hadn't given it much thought," he said. "It's like the girl you never think about dating, but then you meet and ... whoa."[49] By the time the season opened in April 2001, Rodriguez realized the huge contract had made him a target for people critical of escalating sports salaries. "There's this 252 tag over my head,"[50] Rodriguez admitted.

He soon acquired insulting new nicknames like "Pay-Rod" and "Mr. 252" and reporters began watching him closely to see if he could perform well enough to earn his astronomical salary.

Tough Times in Texas

The Texas Rangers opened their 2001 season in San Juan, Puerto Rico, against the Toronto Blue Jays. The April 1 game was part of baseball's attempt to grow interest in the sport internationally by playing games outside the United States. But Rodriguez was the focus of attention because of his contract. Rodriguez singled in his first at bat for Texas and added a double later, but the Rangers lost 8–1. And because he slipped and fell down while attempting a double play, some reporters said it showed he was not worth all the money he was being paid. It did not get any easier for Rodriguez when the Rangers began a series in Seattle on April 16. Mariners fans, angry that he left to make more money with the Rangers, booed Rodriguez, held signs saying "Pay Rod," and showered the field with fake dollar bills.

Rodriguez managed to live up to his new status as the nation's highest-paid athlete, and he withstood the accompanying criticism from fans and the news media. He had another outstanding season as he hit .318 and led the league with 52 home runs. On September 28, when he became the first shortstop to hit 50 home runs in a season, he explained how proud he was: "This means a lot, with the history of this game and all. It's very flattering and I feel very humbled by the accomplishment. Hopefully, I can do it in a season that's a lot more gratifying for me and the team."[51] Rodriguez's accomplishments were overshadowed,

Chicago Cubs Hall-of-Fame shortstop Ernie Banks called Rodriguez the best shortstop ever, but the Rangers' losses kept piling up, and Rodriguez was embarrassed.

however, because the team was losing despite his spectacular play. The Rangers were playing terribly because of poor pitching and finished in last place with a 73–89 record.

The Rangers would also finish last in 2002—they were one game worse at 72–90—despite another extraordinary season of play by Rodriguez, who led the American League with a career-high 57 home runs and 142 RBI. He was so good that Chicago Cubs hall-of-fame shortstop Ernie Banks said in September that Rodriguez was the best shortstop ever. "To me, he is," said Banks. "To see this young man play that position with power and his defensive ability, it's really, really exceptional."[52]

The continual losing began to bother Rodriguez. After the Kansas City Royals beat the Rangers 8–6 and 6–4 in two straight games he admitted, "This is embarrassing. We should all be embarrassed. Basically, we are a failure. It's embarrassing to me to not help the team and contribute more."[53] Even though team officials did not blame Rodriguez, he felt bad about losing so many games while being paid so much money. The news media and fans added to his frustration by blaming him, even though wiser people knew that it takes more than one great player to win in baseball.

Even as Rodriguez suffered through another losing season, his private life became much happier when he married his long-time girlfriend, Cynthia Scurtis.

Happy off the Field

The couple was married on November 2, 2002, by Scurtis's grandfather, Demosthenes Mekras, a Greek Orthodox priest. For the sake of privacy, the ceremony was held at Rodriguez's home in Highland Park, Texas. Texas Rangers owner Tom Hicks, who treated Rodriguez well during the three seasons he played for the Rangers, hosted the rehearsal dinner the day before the wedding at his own home. He believed Cynthia, who was working as a pretrial counselor for poor and underprivileged defendants, was good for Rodriguez. He said, "She was the rock in their relationship. I think she helped him be a man."[54]

Rodriguez had all the money anyone could ever need. Although he bought cars and boats and other luxury items, he also gave a lot of money to charity. In 1996 Rodriguez founded Grand Slam for Kids, an educational program that encouraged grade-school children to work on their studies and learn good citizenship, and two years later he started the Alex Rodriguez Family Foundation, which raises funds for several charities. He was also the national

In 2002, Rodriguez married Cynthia Scurtis in a private ceremony in Texas.

spokesperson for the Boys & Girls Clubs of America, which had helped him when he was young and hosted an annual dinner for the clubs in Miami. Rodriguez said it felt good to help others after having grown up poor himself. He explains, "I really enjoy being involved in the community and doing some philanthropy, both in Dallas and the Miami area, as well as in the Dominican Republic. I feel it's an obligation. I really do. I've been incredibly fortunate, and I feel an incredible amount of privilege to give back."[55]

In 2002 Rodriguez also gave something back to the University of Miami, the school he almost attended before signing with the Seattle Mariners. On October 10, Rodriguez pledged to give the school $3.9 million over six years to strengthen the school's baseball program. He said as a child he used to sneak into the university's Mark Light Field, where he would run the bases and pretend he was playing there. "In South Florida, this is what we had," Rodriguez said at a news conference at the school. "So it's a very dear, special place to me."[56] A big part of his donation was dedicated to renovating the stadium. Renovations were completed in 2009 and the stadium was renamed Alex Rodriguez Park.

Despite getting married and doing charitable work, Rodriguez devoted most of his off-season to preparing for his third year with the Rangers. And in 2003 his hard work paid off like never before.

An MVP Season

In 2003 the Rangers finished in last place for the fourth straight year with a 71–91 record. The presence of the highest-paid player in baseball—his $22-million-a-year salary was more money than the entire Tampa Bay Devil Rays team made—had failed again to help the team improve. But the 2003 season, even more than the first two seasons, proved Rodriguez was not to blame for the team's woeful play as he continued his outstanding individual performance and assault on baseball's record books.

An example of how one player cannot make an entire team win games came on April 2 when Rodriguez hit his three hundredth

An MVP Award

The Baseball Writers' Association of America presents the Most Valuable Player (MVP) award annually in the American League and National League. Most MVPs are selected from winning teams, so it was rare when Alex Rodriguez won in 2003 because he played for a team that finished with a 71–91 record and in last place in its division. Andre Dawson, the 1987 National League MVP for the Chicago Cubs, is the only other winner who played for a last place team. Rodriguez is one of ten players who has won the award three times. He also captured it in 2005 and 2007—and has been a strong candidate for it in several other years. In 2003 Rodriguez received 242 points to beat Toronto Blue Jays first baseman Carlos Delgado, who had 213 points, and New York Yankees catcher Jorge Posada who was third with 194. (Members of the Baseball Writers Association rank their top ten MVP candidates, each first place vote getting ten points, each second place nine points, etc. The points are added up to see who received the award.) In 2002 Rodriguez finished second in voting to Miguel Tejada of the Oakland A's and in 1996 he lost by only 3 points to Juan Gonzalez of the Rangers. After two near misses, Rodriguez was happy to finally win:

"I almost forgot about the date. Other years I'd be sitting by the phone praying. I felt I was driving myself crazy over this award. To take away the pain, I told myself if you come in second or third, mission accomplished. But obviously winning it is great."

Quoted in Rafael Hermoso, "Rodriguez Wins M.V.P. as Trade Talks Swirl." *New York Times*, November 18, 2003.

career home run to become the youngest player to reach that milestone at 27 years, 249 days old. The fastest to hit three hundred previously at 27 years, 328 days was hall of famer Jimmie Foxx, who finished his career with 534 homers. Despite Rodriguez's historic three-run homer, the Rangers lost 11–5 to the Los Angeles Angels. And the Rangers kept losing despite the

Rodriguez was named MVP in 2003. Despite his team's last place finish, A-Rod himself had a great year.

fact that Rodriguez had a career-high 57 home runs, more than any player in the American or National Leagues, and 142 RBI.

Rodriguez's season was so sensational that in November he won the American League Most Valuable Player (MVP) award, the highest honor a player can receive. Although Rodriguez was ecstatic about winning the award, he admitted in a news conference that "it's been a rough three years in Texas." Rodriguez had seven years left on his historic contract, but he pointed out that they might not be spent with the Rangers because the team had begun talking with other teams about trading him. Rodriguez had the right to veto a trade he did not like, but he said he had told the Rangers he was willing to be flexible about any deal the team worked out. "I did not approach management, management approached me,"[57] Rodriguez says. But he had begun to realize as early as July, when he was heading to his seventh All-Star Game while the Rangers were slipping toward their fourth consecutive last place finish in the American League West Division, that the team might be better off using the huge salary it was paying him to pay several new players instead to strengthen the team. He told reporters, "If the Rangers found they could be better off without me—whether now or a year or two down the road—I'd be willing to sit down and talk. I want what's best for Mr. Hicks."[58]

Even though team owner Tom Hicks had said Rodriguez was a valuable asset to the team and did not want to trade him, sportswriters had begun writing that a trade would be best for both Rodriguez and the Rangers. *USA Today* sports columnist Jon Saraceno noted that it was sad that one of the best players in baseball was stuck on such a horrible team. In a 2003 article he writes that Rodriguez was probably the "unhappiest $250 Million Man in sports" and claims "A-Rod is A-Rotting away in Texas. But for how long?"[59] Saraceno contended that it was only a matter of time before the Rangers realized they should trade Rodriguez.

As it turned out, Rodriguez would not have long to wait for that to happen. A trade after the 2004 season would send him back to the city of his birth—New York.

Chapter 5

A New York Yankee

By the end of the 2003 season, Texas Rangers owner Tom Hicks knew that trading Rodriguez was the only way to improve his team. A trade would give the Rangers several good players for one great one while also freeing up cash that it could use to sign even more players. Only a few teams, however, had enough money to pay the last seven years of Rodriguez's $252 million contract. When a deal with the Boston Red Sox fell through in December, the Rangers began talking with the New York Yankees. After extended negotiations that included Rodriguez and his agent, Scott Boras, the teams finalized one of the biggest trades in baseball history.

Rodriguez Returns to New York

On February 16, 2004, the Rangers sent Rodriguez to the Yankees in exchange for two infielders: major league star Alfonso Soriano and minor league player Joaquin Arias. The Rangers also agreed to pay part of Rodriguez's salary through 2010, when the contract ended, including $3 million in 2004. Rodriguez was delighted with the deal, because he had always loved New York City and he would be playing for a team that had won more World Series than any other—twenty-six, including four from 1996 through 2000. In a news conference Rodriguez said it was a dream come true to play for the Yankees. But he also said he had another reason for joining the Yankees: "To me, it was a very easy decision. To me, this came down to winning."[60]

But to realize his dream of playing for the Yankees, Rodriguez had to agree to switch positions. Yankees owner George Steinbrenner demanded that Rodriguez move to third base so Derek Jeter, the team's acknowledged leader, could continue playing short-stop. Rodriguez accepted the position switch even though he was considered the best shortstop in baseball. He was willing to make this compromise, because he really wanted to play for the Yankees and because he and Jeter had been good friends since meeting years earlier in an orientation session for major league rookies. In 2001 Jeter described his friendship with Rodriguez to a reporter. He said, "We spend lot of time together, especially in the off-season. He comes over to my house [in Florida] for New Year's. Every opportunity we get to do things together, we

In 2004, the Rangers had to trade Rodriguez in exchange for several other good players. Rodriguez returned to his childhood home of New York City to play for the Yankees.

Traded to the Yankees

In 2003 the Texas Rangers found it difficult to trade Alex Rodriguez because the team owed him $179 million for the last seven years of his contract. In early December, however, the Rangers agreed to trade Rodriguez to the Boston Red Sox for hard-hitting Manny Ramirez and minor league pitching prospect Jon Lester. Rodriguez agreed to the trade even though the Red Sox demanded that his contract be restructured. When the Major League Players Association withheld its approval because Rodriguez would receive less money, the New York Yankees were able to sign Rodriguez. At a news conference on February 17, 2004, Yankee great Reggie Jackson ridiculed the Red Sox for valuing money over a great player. He said,

> They had a greater need [for Rodriguez] than money. Twelve million [dollars] is huge for normal people but not the people running baseball, especially when it comes to arguably the best player in the game. It's not about winning 112 or 114 regular-season games around here, it's about winning eleven games in the post-season. You need guys that will help you win the last eleven games. We [the Yankees] were the only team in baseball with the balls to pull this off and take the chance.

Quoted in Mike Vaccaro, *Emperors and Idiots: The Hundred-Year Rivalry Between the Yankees and Red Sox, From the Very Beginning to the End of the Curse.* New York: Doubleday, 2005, p. 186.

do, so he really is like a brother."[61] Rodriguez had always publicly praised Jeter's ability as a shortstop. But Rodriguez had also envied the four World Series that Jeter had won with the Yankees, and his desperate desire to have his own World Series win made the switch easier to accept.

Rodriguez had to give up one more thing to become a Yankee—his uniform number. He had always worn number three in baseball, but the Yankees had retired that number in honor of legendary player Babe Ruth. So Rodriguez began wearing number thirteen, the number he had worn as a high school quarterback in honor of Miami Dolphins quarterback Dan Marino.

Playing as a Yankee

From 2005 through 2008, Rodriguez remained one of the best and most popular players in baseball. Proof of his stellar play was that he won two more Most Valuable Player (MVP) awards in 2005 and 2007. In 2005 Rodriguez hit .321 with 48 home runs and 130 runs batted in (RBI) and was the first Yankee to lead the American League in home runs since Reggie Jackson hit 41 in 1980. Rodriguez also hit 26 home runs that season in Yankee Stadium, breaking the team's home record of 25 homers which was shared by Joe DiMaggio and Gary Sheffield. And in 2007 Rodriguez hit .314 with 54 homers and 156 RBI as he continued his assault on baseball's all-time records. On August 4, 2007, Rodriguez smashed the first pitch from Kyle Davies of the Kansas City Royals into the left-field stands at Yankee Stadium to become the twenty-second player and youngest ever to hit 500 home runs. The homer came eight days after his thirty-second birthday.

From 2005 to 2008 the Yankees finished first in the American League East Division three times and second and third once each. During this period, the team won as many as forty more games than they lost each season—their 2004 record was 101–61—but only captured one American League title (2003) and failed to win a World Series championship. Although Rodriguez was a star during the regular season, he slumped badly in postseason play when championships were at stake. In his MVP season in 2005, Rodriguez had just two hits and no RBI when the Los Angeles Angels eliminated the Yankees in a first-round playoff. Even Rodriguez admitted, "I played like a dog."[62] Rodriguez floundered just as badly in 2006 as he managed only four hits and no RBI in another first-round playoff loss to the Detroit Tigers.

Because the Yankees player payroll exceeded $200 million, by far the most of any major league team, the team was ridiculed for failing to do better in the postseason. Even though Jeter and several other Yankees made nearly as much as Rodriguez, his historic contract made him a target for fans and reporters upset about the Yankees's lack of postseason success. In October 2006 sportswriter Norman Chad wrote that it was not fair to blame Rodriguez for those failures:

> A-Rod has been a perfect citizen, a drug-free, scandal-free superstar who doesn't embarrass himself, his teammates or his family. He plays hard every day. And his reward for this? This year, he's been booed at home, vilified on sports radio, torched by the New York tabloids [and even been] called E-Rod, K-Rod and A-Fraud.[63]

Rodriguez had always enjoyed the kind of clean image Chad describes. He had done very few things wrong publicly except to play poorly in clutch situations (critical game situations that help determine whether the game is won or lost). But his image of personal perfection began to tarnish in New York as the public began learning about some of the negative things he was doing.

Clubhouse Trouble

Joe Torre was the Yankees's manager from 1996 to 2007, when he was fired because of the team's postseason flops. In a 2009 book about his years with the Yankees, Torre criticizes Rodriguez for always trying to be the center of media attention and accused him of caring more about his individual achievements than whether the team won games. "We never really had anybody who craved the attention," Torre wrote, "[and] seeing his personality concerned me because you could see his focus was on individual stuff."[64]

Rodriguez's reputation had already been damaged in 2003 when newspaper stories at that time reported problems Rodriguez had getting along with Rangers' manager Buck Showalter and his teammates, who thought he tried to act like a big shot. Even Hicks, who had always supported Rodriguez, admitted several years later that "in our clubhouse back then, Alex kind of sucked

Rodriguez, left, had strained relations with his new team members, including his old friend Derek Jeter, right. Despite the team's winning performance, Rodriguez almost lost his contract with the Yankees.

the air out of the room and didn't leave air for other people."[65] Baseball clubhouses have several attendants who bring the players fresh towels and other supplies and run errands for them. When he was with the Rangers, Rodriguez demanded that one of the clubhouse attendants be assigned solely to him.

Some Yankees players did not like Rodriguez when he arrived because he seemed vain. When Rodriguez hit a home run, players said he would ask them how he looked while hitting it, as if he was seeking compliments. His teammates were also bothered by an incident in 2004 in Houston, Texas. During his trip there in July for the All-Star Game, Rodriguez held a news conference and announced he was opening a Mercedes-Benz dealership in the Houston area. His teammates thought he was wrong to have combined personal business with an occasion meant to honor the game of baseball.

A-Fraud

When Alex Rodriguez joined the New York Yankees in 2004, some of his new teammates called him A-Fraud behind his back. They thought he was insincere in trying to become friends with them, and they resented him because he always tried to attract attention to himself. When Rodriguez was on base he would

When A-Rod first started playing for the Yankees, some team members gave him the name A-Fraud because they thought he was insincere.

point to outfielders to show he knew where they were positioned, something base runners need to know. But by pointing he seemed to be showing off to fans. Mike Borzello, the team's bullpen coach and a close friend of Rodriguez, explains:

He *was* phony, and he knew he was phony. But he didn't know how to be anything else at that time. Then he started to realize what it's all about and what people feed off of, and thought, "Hey, I can really be myself." I used to tell Alex all the time, I said, "You come to the stadium and you try to get everyone to look at you. Meanwhile, they already are looking at you. You're Alex Rodriguez. I don't understand that." And he would say, "Well, I like to play with a certain style." I said, "You do things on the field that draw attention to yourself that are unnecessary, and you want people to know how good you are, how smart a baseball player you are. And we already know that. Just play, stop saying, 'Look at me.' We're already looking."

Quoted in Joe Torre and Tom Verducci, *The Yankee Years.* New York: Doubleday, 2009, pp. 245–246.

A-Rod's tenuous relationships with other Yankees included Jeter. Their longtime friendship was first weakened by comments Rodriguez made in a 2001 magazine article that were critical of Jeter. He tried to diminish his friend's achievements as a Yankee by claiming that Jeter held an advantage by playing on a stronger team than Rodriguez, who was with the lowly Rangers. Even though Rodriguez later apologized for his remarks, the incident strained their friendship. And when they became teammates, the two perennial all-star players were never as friendly toward each other as Rodriguez claimed when he signed with the team.

Torre writes about the tension between the two stars in his book and cites one incident in which they let an infield pop fly fall between them instead of working together to catch it. Their mutual resentment seemed to be the reason neither tried to catch the ball, which made Torre scold them. "I don't know who wants to catch that thing, but *somebody* has to catch [it],"[66] he told them after the game while warning them to work together on such plays. The relationship was so hostile that in 2007 Rodriguez finally commented about it. "Get over it. We're no longer that great of friends,"[67] he told reporters.

During the 2007 season, Rodriguez further alienated his teammates and Yankees management by negotiating a new contract. A clause in the contract gave Rodriguez the right to opt out after seven years. He did that even though he was still making more money than any other player. In October when Boras told Yankees management that Rodriguez wanted a new ten-year, $350-million contract, the Yankees responded that they would not pay that much.

The Yankees response frightened Rodriguez because he knew no other team could pay him as much money as the Yankees. So he and his wife, Cynthia, met in Florida with brothers Hal and Hank Steinbrenner, who were managing the team for their dad. With Rodriguez acting contrite, the couple convinced the Steinbrenners to keep Rodriguez. Negotiations with Boras resumed and on December 17 Rodriguez signed a ten-year contract for $275 million with incentives that could push the total to $305 million. He later commented on his reaction to the Yankees decision not to sign him:

I woke up the next morning and I was white as a ghost. My want was always to become a world champion in New York. I have a lot to prove in New York. . . . The whole thing was a mistake. It was a huge debacle. It was very stressful, and to me it was a very humbling experience. I made a huge mistake.[68]

The mistake Rodriguez made in negotiating with the Yankees was not the only one he made during this period. His private life was also suffering because of his actions.

Personal Struggles

Rodriguez's image had always been that of a hardworking player, who was a loving husband and father to his two daughters—Natasha Alexander, born on February 15, 2004, and Ella Alexander, born on April 21, 2008. During spring training in 2008, a New York Yankees television network show called *YESterdays* featured Rodriguez. Appearing on the show with him were his siblings and his wife, Cynthia, who was pregnant with Ella.

The show was repeated over and over for a month and further strengthened Rodriguez's image as a good family man. But only five months later, on July 7, Cynthia filed papers for divorce. She accused Rodriguez of infidelity after newspaper stories linked him with a Las Vegas stripper and with rock star Madonna. Newspaper reports also claimed that during 2006 and 2007 he had paid for sex with New York prostitutes. A month later Rodriguez filed a response to the divorce petition that stated, "Husband denies any duty to support wife beyond those obligations specifically set out in the parties' prenuptial agreement and Florida law."[69] Because Rodriguez was so wealthy, the statement further sullied his reputation by making him look cheap toward a wife he had cheated on.

His sexual escapades were only one way in which Rodriguez's lifestyle had changed since moving to New York. Rodriguez also began playing poker and hosting charity poker tournaments

Along with difficulties on the Yankees, Rodriguez's personal life also began to suffer. He was reported to be having an affair with pop star Madonna, and his wife filed for divorce.

for large sums of money for which he was criticized. Rodriguez shrugged off the criticism by saying he was just trying to relax and have fun. After a game in September in Seattle, Rodriguez

Alex Rodriguez Talks About Therapy

On May 27, 2005, the American Academy of Child and Adolescent Psychiatry issued a statement praising Alex Rodriguez for publicly talking about psychological therapy he received to deal with some psychological problems. The group said his openness would make it easier for children and other people to get help when they needed it. Rodriguez had made the admission a few days earlier after he and his wife gave two hundred thousand dollars to a mental health program at the Children's Aid Society in Washington Heights, the New York neighborhood he lived in as a small child. His wife, a psychologist, convinced him to see several therapists to deal with some emotional issues, such as his feelings about being abandoned by his father when he was nine years old. Mental illness is something most people, including athletes, are afraid to talk about. But according to Rodriguez, therapy helped him. He says,

I don't know where I'd be. I think it's a different life that I've discovered and I thank Cynthia for that because therapy is an incredible thing and you might get to know someone you didn't even know was in there. Why let the train wreck come before you fix it? It's helped in baseball, for one, in terms of my approach to everything. I think it would be great if kids out there realize that it can be a great benefit.

Quoted in Sam Borden and Corky Siemaszko, "Rodriguez Steps Up, Praises Therapy." *New York Daily News*, May 24, 2005.

commented cynically that when he acted "perfectly" while playing for the Mariners everybody loved him but "now I'm not perfect and I love it."[70]

Some people believe the change in Rodriguez's lifestyle could be linked to his move to New York. In discussing Rodriguez, teammate Gary Sheffield said, "He's a good boy, but New York offered him a lot of temptation. A bite of the Big Apple [New York's nickname] is fine. You eat it all, and it's too much."[71]

Although his personal image suffered, Rodriguez remained popular as a player. One reason was that he was one of the few power-hitting stars who had not been linked to steroid use. Just a few months before Rodriguez and his wife filmed *YESterdays*, they had a joint appearance on the television show *60 Minutes*. During the interview, CBS anchor Katie Couric asked Rodriguez if he had ever been tempted to use steroids to build up strength and endurance. He replied, "No. I've never felt overmatched on the baseball field. I've always been a very strong, dominant position. And I felt that if I did my work as I've done since I was, you know, a rookie back in Seattle, I didn't have a problem competing at any level. So, no."[72]

But Rodriguez lied. And in 2009 when a sports magazine revealed he had used steroids, he was thrown into the biggest crisis of his baseball career.

Chapter 6

Dishonor and Redemption

On February 7, 2009, Alex Rodriguez was working out in the weight room at the University of Miami gym when *Sports Illustrated* reporter Selena Roberts approached him and began asking some difficult questions. To Rodriguez's dismay, Roberts told Rodriguez she knew that in 2003 when he played for the Texas Rangers, he had tested positive for two anabolic steroids, testosterone and Primobolan. Rodriguez tried to brush her off by saying, "You'll have to talk to the [players] union" but when Roberts tried to question him further he told her "I'm not saying anything."[73] When Roberts continued seeking answers to her questions, Rodriguez asked the gym staff to order the reporter out of the gym. Roberts gave Rodriguez her card, asked him to call her if he wanted to answer questions, and left.

That same day Roberts and coauthor David Epstein filed a story on *Sports Illustrated*'s website with details about Rodriguez's positive test for steroids, a performance enhancing drug (PED) banned in all sports because it gives athletes an unfair advantage over their competitors. Thus began the most humiliating and stressful period in Rodriguez's life.

The Steroid Scandal

As Roberts had learned, Rodriguez was 1 of 104 players who had positive results out of 1,198 players who were tested for steroids in 2003. Although Major League Baseball had prohibited PEDs

In 2009, reporter questioned Rodriguez, now with the New York Yankees, about his testing positive for steroid use back in 2003 when he played for the Texas Rangers (left).

since 1971, it did not begin test players until 2003. The league had been lax for decades in policing the drugs, even though players like Jose Canseco, Mark McGwire, and Barry Bonds had long been suspected of using them. The suspicions arose because, like Rodriguez, they had such muscular physiques and hit so many home runs. The 2003 tests were supposedly a confidential and anonymous way for the league to test players and see if future random drug testing might be necessary. The players who tested positive were not punished and Major League Baseball did not institute penalties for steroid users until the 2006 season.

Steroid use by Bonds and other players had made headlines for several years before Roberts obtained the 2003 results. When her story about Rodriguez was published, other news media quickly picked it up, and it became a media sensation. Two days after the story was posted on the Internet, Rodriguez admitted in an ESPN interview that he had used steroids from 2001 to 2003. Rodriguez said he used steroids so he could play well enough to justify his $252 million contract with the Rangers:

Rodriguez's Steroid Use

After Selena Roberts coauthored the *Sports Illustrated* magazine story in 2009 that revealed Alex Rodriguez's steroid use, she wrote a biography about Rodriguez. In the book, Roberts speculates that Rodriguez had used steroids before the three-year period (2001–2003) in which he admitted using them. Claiming that "the arc that traces Alex Rodriguez's rise to superstardom neatly parallels the one tracking the abuse of steroids in baseball," Roberts argues that steroids might have helped Rodriguez gain 25 pounds (11kg) between his sophomore and junior years in high school. To support that contention, Roberts discusses his friendship with Jose Canseco, one of the first players who admitted to using steroids. Canseco, who was born in Cuba but grew up in Miami, befriended the younger Rodriguez when he was in high school. They worked out together, and Roberts believes that Canseco could have taught him about taking steroids to improve performance. Roberts quotes Canseco on Rodriguez's possible steroid use: "Was he on steroids in high school? I think probably so. I worked out with him when he was 18. He could lift as much as I could." In 1988 Canseco was the first player to hit forty home runs and steal forty bases, showing he had a phenomenal combination of speed and power. Rodriguez and Barry Bonds are the only other two players to match that record and both used steroids.

Selena Roberts, *A-Rod: The Many Lives of Alex Rodriguez*. New York: HarperCollins, 2009, p. 102.

When I arrived in Texas in 2001, I felt an enormous amount of pressure. I felt like I had all the weight of the world on top of me, and I needed to perform, and perform at a high level every day. [I] just feel that, you know, I'm just sorry. I'm sorry for that time. I'm sorry to my fans. I'm sorry for my fans in Texas. It wasn't until then that I ever thought about a substance of any kind, and since then, I've proved to myself and to everyone that I don't need any of that.[74]

Rodriguez's admission angered his fans and Rangers owner Tom Hicks, who said he had never suspected Rodriguez took steroids. "In fact," Hicks said, "Alex used to tell me negative things about other players around the league who were suspected [of using steroids]. So it's ... I feel very betrayed."[75] Rodriguez's contrite confession did not quell the media firestorm that engulfed him. On February 17, Rodriguez was even more open about his steroid use when reporters questioned him at the New York Yankees' spring training site in Tampa, Florida. He admitted that while he was with the Rangers, he had injected himself with the drug twice a month for six months each year to build strength and endurance.

Yankees manager Joe Girardi said Rodriguez's second admission of steroid use was more dramatic and painful than the first because it came in front of his teammates. "I saw tears in his eyes," Girardi said. "For him to look over and see his teammates, he was moved. I think he really felt like they were part of his family." Girardi predicted that it would take time for Rodriguez to win back the affection of fans: "I think a lot of people are going to say, 'Prove it to me.' That's what happens when trust is broken."[76]

Rodriguez knew that he had to show fans and critics that he was still a great player even though he was no longer taking steroids. But his season of redemption got off to a slow start because of an injury.

A Better Attitude

During spring training in 2009, doctors discovered torn cartilage in Rodriguez's right leg. Surgery to repair it took place on March 9. Because it took nine weeks to heal and get back into playing shape, Rodriguez missed the first six weeks of the regular season. He returned to action on May 8 and hit a three-run home run on the first pitch thrown to him. The run powered the Yankees to a 4–0 victory over the Baltimore Orioles. Teammate Johnny Damon said that when Rodriguez came back, more than his injured knee had been healed. According to Damon, the time Rodriguez spent recuperating from surgery enabled him to develop a better attitude toward baseball and his teammates. Damon explains,

A coach helps Rodriguez warm up before a game shortly after he returned to the field after having surgery.

I think he wants to please all the guys in here—produce on the baseball field, do what he knows and finally be himself. For so long, he was trying to be this person that made everyone happy and tried to be the guy who pleased everyone, and now I think he's No. 1. He wants to make sure he's in a good spot, because if he's in a good spot, the rest of us are, too.[77]

After struggling to a 13–15 record without Rodriguez, the Yankees began winning again when he returned to the lineup. His injury limited Rodriguez to 124 games, his lowest total since becoming a starter in 1996, but he batted .286, smashed 35 home runs, and had 103 runs batted in (RBI) to help the Yankees to the best record in baseball at 103–59. Midway through the season Rodriguez admitted, "I'm having a blast."[78] He had put the steroid abuse issue behind him and was in top form. And blasts—a nickname for home runs—played a prominent part in his renewed joy in playing. Rodriguez finished the season with 583 homers to tie Mark McGwire for eighth place for career home runs. In August Rodriguez explained why he was having so much fun and doing so well despite the negative start to his season: "I took a lot of things off my chest and, to me, since that press conference [with ESPN] I felt like a new man. I feel like I've been embraced by not only the city of New York, but my teammates, my coaches and my manager. I just feel liberated by just the way I came out and did things."[79]

Rodriguez capped his historic season on October 4 by hitting two home runs in one inning to drive in seven runs and set an American League record for the most RBI in one inning. Such play helped Rodriguez lead the Yankees into the postseason. But after years of postseason failure, Rodriguez still had to prove he could play like a star when a championship was at stake.

A Postseason Hero

Since Game 4 of the 2004 American League Championship Series, Rodriguez had batted sixty-one times in playoff games while failing to drive in any of the thirty-eight runners who had been on base. His inability to produce runs was the main reason Rodriguez had been harshly criticized by fans and the media. But in the first game of the 2009 American League Division Series against the Minnesota Twins, Rodriguez stroked two RBI singles, and in the second game he had an RBI single and a home run to show that he was not going to be another postseason flop.

In the World Series between the Yankees and the Philadelphia Phillies, Rodriguez—labeled the Playoff Monster for his great performance—hit a game-winning two-run home run.

Rodriguez had a pair of home runs and drove in six runs to help the Yankees win the five game series 3–0.

The Yankees then faced the Los Angeles Angels in the championship series for the right to advance to the World Series. Rodriguez played masterfully again with three home runs and six RBI that helped New York beat the Angels 4–2 in a seven-game series. His ninth inning home run in game two tied the score at 3–3 and allowed the Yankees to go to extra innings and win 4–3 for a commanding 2–0 series lead.

Rodriguez was playing so well that one news story about his heroics labeled him a "Playoff Monster." Fans and even Yankee great Reggie Jackson, who was called by the nickname "Mr. October" because he helped the Yankees win so many playoff games (which occur mostly in October) during his hall-of-fame

Rodriguez Assesses His 2009 Season

On February 25, 2010, Alex Rodriguez spoke to reporters during spring training. The news conference was in stark contrast to the one a year earlier in which Rodriguez had been forced to admit he used steroids while with the Texas Rangers. In 2010 a much happier Rodriguez discussed how he had dealt with the shameful part of his past since then and went on to become a World Series hero. Here are excerpts from his news conference:

It's obviously a very different day. Last year was a very embarrassing day, something I wouldn't want to go back and do. But looking back, I thought it was a very important day. It was the most difficult day of my life, if not, definitely one of the top three....

Experiencing a World Championship in New York [is] something I will never forget. It was a magical feeling....

It wasn't a monkey—it was a humongous gorilla that came off my back [to finally have a great postseason]. It was a heavy gorilla. Now, I have an opportunity to just come out and play baseball....

[2009] was a year I'll probably understand twenty or thirty years from now, all the things that transpired in one year. From as low as any person or athlete could probably get to where we ended up in early November, it's something I'm in awe of. I couldn't believe it was me it was happening to.

Quoted in Dom Amore, "Alex Rodriguez: In His Own Words," *Hartford Courant*, February 25, 2010, http://blogs.courant.com/baseball/2010/02/alex-rodriguez-in-his-own-word.html.

career, were excited about Rodriguez. "It's wonderful to see," Jackson said. "I'm diggin' it. It's like watching a star in a movie. We all knew he had it in him. And when you see it come out like this, there's a real joy in it."[80]

The World Series pitted the Yankees against the Philadelphia Phillies, a team that had won the 2008 championship. The Phillies won the first game 6–1 on a masterful pitching performance by Cliff Lee, but the Yankees took the second game 3–1 and also won the third game 8–5 thanks to another historic Rodriguez home run. In the fourth inning Rodriguez hit a long fly ball into the right-field stands that was ruled a double because umpires believed it had bounced into the stands. But instant replay reversed the call when it showed that the ball hit a camera and then flew into the stands for a two-run homer. It was the first instant replay review in World Series history.

In the ninth inning of game four, Rodriguez smashed a game-winning double deep into left field to lift the Yankees to a 7–4 victory and a commanding 3–1 series lead. Although Rodriguez downplayed his heroics, saying, "I'm just trying to swing at strikes," Damon claimed Rodriguez was why the Yankees were one victory away from a championship: "He's the reason we're sitting here and we're in Philadelphia right now. I feel like without him who knows where our road show would have stopped."[81]

The Yankees went on to win the series 4–2 for their twenty-seventh World Series win. Rodriguez played a huge role in the championship. In its commemorative issue on the championship *Sports Illustrated*—the magazine that caused Rodriguez so much grief by revealing his steroid use months earlier—titled an article on Rodriguez "Mr. November." That take-off on Jackson's "Mr. October" nickname was the highest form of praise the magazine could have given Rodriguez.

By the end of the season, in addition to being more comfortable on the field, Rodriguez was also more content in his private life.

Happier Times

Marital problems and divorce are difficult for anyone, but they can be especially difficult for celebrities, whose every move is documented by the news media. Newspapers in 2008 were filled with stories about Rodriguez's marital problems and his divorce, which was finalized that September. But in 2009, newspapers reported happier news when Rodriguez began dating actress Kate Hudson. They began seeing each other at the beginning of the year, and in July at a team picnic Rodriguez confirmed they were a couple. They even began having dates in public that included his daughters, four-year-old Natasha and one-year-old Ella, and Hudson's son, five-year-old Ryder. Some reporters speculated that the romance made Rodriguez so happy that it was the reason his batting average rose 54 points to .310 in the second half of the season.

Rodriguez catches a foul ball while actress Kate Hudson, right, looks on. The baseball player and actress later dated.

Rodriguez had always been involved in charitable and community events. But Ray Negron, who schedules community events for Yankee players, notes that during the 2009 season, Rodriguez increased his community work. Negron described one incident in particular that he thought showed Rodriguez's new

Shortstop Legacy

One of Alex Rodriguez's baseball legacies will be his influence on what kind of athletes will play shortstop in the future. For decades, shortstops were usually the smallest player on the team, like Freddie Patek, a three-time Kansas City all-star in the 1970s who was 5 feet, 5 inches (1.7m) tall. They were often weak hitters as well because teams spent more time training them to be good shortstops than good hitters. But in the 1980s Cal Ripken Jr. proved that a bigger player who could hit for power could field that position. That led to big, hard-hitting shortstops in the 1990s like Rodriguez and Derek Jeter of the New York Yankees. Baseball writer Evan Grant claims Rodriguez helped change future expectations for shortstops:

> What sets Rodriguez apart is his advanced placement on the shortstop's evolutionary chart. He is the successor to those quick, agile shortstops of the 1970s. His love of the game makes him the successor to Ernie Banks' "Let's play two" persona. [Hall of Fame player Ernie Banks was a shortstop and first baseman for the Chicago Cubs.] His knowledge of the game makes him the successor to the day when the shortstop was considered prime managerial material. He is Ripken's successor as an elegant man, an intelligent player and a feared hitter. "Cal meant an awful lot to me," Rodriguez said. "He gave me the feeling that it could be done, that I could play shortstop at my size. Hopefully, we can do the same for some kids out there today. Hopefully, we can open up avenues for the next generation."

Evan Grant, "Texas' Alex Rodriguez: A Complete Package of Talent." *Baseball Digest*, March 2002, p. 24.

attitude: "There's a difference in Alex this year, by far. One day he went out to play stickball in the streets in the Bronx with the kids, unannounced. Before you knew it, there were kids running from every direction, every block. They loved it."[82]

After the 2009 season, Rodriguez and Hudson broke up, but he was soon dating actress Cameron Diaz. As always, Rodriguez spent the off-season in Miami, which allowed him to train hard and spend more time with his children, who lived there with his ex-wife. When Rodriguez reported for training camp, he was healthier and happier than he had been a year earlier when the steroid scandal erupted. Rodriguez talked candidly to reporters about how his experiences in 2009 had changed him:

> Last year, obviously, was very embarrassing. It [the day of the steroid news conference] was the most difficult day of my life. Looking back, it was a necessary step. I had hit rock bottom. I took that time to look in the mirror and be honest with myself. I've done a lot of growing up. Now, it's my responsibility to continue that.[83]

His comments indicated that the tough times Rodriguez went through had produced a new maturity, which was fitting because in July 2010 he celebrated his thirty-fifth birthday. No longer the young star, he was an established veteran heading into the final years of an illustrious career. And in 2010 people began to wonder what Rodriguez's standing will be in comparison to other great players when he is finally done playing baseball.

Rodriguez's Legacy

Rodriguez already held many baseball records. On August 4, 2010, he hit his 600th home run in a game against the Toronto Blue Jays at Yankee Stadium to become only the seventh player to reach that milestone. Rodriguez, who turned 35 on July 27, was the youngest player to hit so many home runs. The fact that he is still in his prime made Rodriguez a likely candidate to break one of baseball's most prized records—career home runs. Barry Bonds holds the record with 762 but if Rodriguez stays healthy and

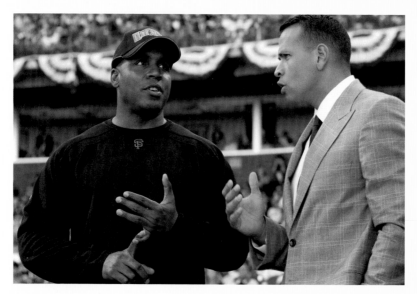

Alex Rodriguez talks with Barry Bonds, left. Rodriguez is well on his way to breaking Bonds' record-holding 762 career home runs.

productive it is estimated that he could surpass 762 in late 2015 or early 2016. The problem for Rodriguez is that if he breaks the record his achievement will be tainted by his steroid use, just as Bonds's home run record is tainted. Another measure of a player's career is whether he is voted into the National Baseball Hall of Fame, located in Cooperstown, Ohio. Rodriguez already has achieved enough to merit that status. But like Bonds, his steroid use may lead sportswriters who vote on hall of fame candidates to leave him off their ballot. Thus, despite the awesome statistics Rodriguez has compiled, his legacy in baseball history remains clouded by some of the controversies of his career.

During spring training in 2010, a reporter asked Rodriguez what he thought his legacy would be. Rodriguez replied: "I don't think about what legacy you have when you're still playing. I think that's something that you consider when your career is over with."[84] If Rodriguez ever does stop and consider his legacy, he might remember something his mother Lourdes once said: "Money and fame are like dust. You aren't worth anything if you don't stay the same person you were before you had them."[85]

Introduction: A Controversial Superstar

1. Quoted in Selena Roberts, *A-Rod: The Many Lives of Alex Rodriguez*. New York: HarperCollins, 2009, p. 91.
2. Quoted in Gerry Callahan, "The Fairest of Them All." *Sports Illustrated*, July 8, 1996, p. 38.
3. Quoted in Bryan Hoch, "A-Rod's Homer an Instant Replay First: Umpires Do Not Change On-Field Call After Using New System," MLB.com, September 4, 2008, http://mlb.mlb.com/news/article.jsp?ymd=20080903&content_id=3416813&vkey=news_mlb&fext=.jsp&c_id=mlb.

Chapter 1: A Difficult Childhood

4. Alex Rodriguez, *Out of the Ballpark*. New York: HarperCollins, 2007.
5. Quoted in Tim Wendel, *The New Face of Baseball: The One-Hundred-Year Rise and Triumph of Latinos in America's Favorite Sport*. New York: HarperCollins, 2003.
6. Quoted in Roberts, *A-Rod*, p. 23.
7. Quoted in Kelly Whiteside, "Alex Rodriguez." *Sports Illustrated*, March 22, 1993, p 74.
8. Quoted in Roberts, *A-Rod*, p. 27.
9. Quoted in Mel Antonen, "Alex Rodriguez: Master of Baseball Arts." *Baseball Digest*, December 2000, p. 36.
10. Quoted in Gerry Callahan, "The Fairest of Them All." *Sports Illustrated*, July 8, 1996, p. 38.
11. Quoted in *Fort Worth Star-Telegram*, "All-Star Rodriguez To Promote Boys & Girls Club." *Fort Worth Star-Telegram*, June 13, 2002.
12. Quoted in Joel Poiley, "Alex Rodriguez: He's with the Club." *Read*, May 9, 2003, p. 13.
13. Quoted in CNN.com, "Alex Rodriguez Profile," CNN.com, www.cnn.com/CNN/Programs/people/shows/rodriguez/profile.html.

14. Quoted in Poiley, "Alex Rodriguez," p. 15.

15. Quoted in Doug Mientkiewicz and Bill Eichenberger, "You Don't Know [Alex Rodriguez] Like I Know [Alex Rodriguez]." *Sporting News*, September 15, 2008, p. 70.

16. Quoted in Whiteside, "Alex Rodriguez," p. 74.

Chapter 2: Becoming a Star

17. Quoted in Roberts, *A-Rod*, p. 54.

18. Quoted in Tim Kurkjian, "Worth Waiting For." *Sports Illustrated*, June 14, 1992, p. 68.

19. Quoted in Whiteside, "Alex Rodriguez," p 74.

20. Quoted in Roberts, *A-Rod*, p. 61.

21. Quoted in William C. Rhoden, "OLYMPICS; Rodriguez a Shortstop with a Long Reach." *New York Times*, July 28, 1993.

22. Quoted in *Fort Worth Star-Telegram*, "Perfect Pursuit: Alex Rodriguez Burns To Be the Best Ever." *Fort Worth Star-Telegram*, July 13, 2002.

23. Quoted in Tom Verducci, "Early Riser: Teenage Sensation Alex Rodriguez Debuted with the Seattle Mariners." *Sports Illustrated*, July 18, 1994, http://sportsillustrated.cnn.com/vault/article/magazine/MAG1005410/index.html.

24. Quoted in Callahan, "The Fairest of Them All," p. 38.

25. Quoted in Jim Street, "Rodriguez Shuttled Back to AAA Tacoma." *Seattle Post-Intelligencer*, August 16, 1995.

26. Quoted in Jimmy Traina, "Timeline Alex Rodriguez." *Sports Illustrated*, http://sportsillustrated.cnn.com/baseball/mlb/features/rodriguez/timeline.

27. Quoted in Callahan, "The Fairest of Them All," p. 38.

28. Quoted in Roberts, *A-Rod*, p. 90.

29. Quoted in Selena Roberts, "Rodriguez, a New Yorker, at Home in Seattle." *New York Times*, August 18, 1996.

30. Quoted in Callahan, "The Fairest of Them All," p. 38.

Chapter 3: The Best Player in Baseball

31. Quoted in Tyler Kepner, "Alex Rodriguez's Talent Has No Boundaries." *Baseball Digest*, May 1999, p. 34.

32. Quoted in Callahan, "The Fairest of Them All," p. 38.

33. Quoted in Murray Chass, "Well Grounded at Shortstop." *New York Times*, March 30, 1997.

34. Quoted in Kepner, "Alex Rodriguez's Talent Has No Boundaries," p. 34.

35. Quoted in Mel Antonen, "Alex Rodriguez: Master of Baseball Arts." *Baseball Digest*, December 2000, p. 36.

36. Quoted in John Hickey, "Mariners' Shortstop Alex Rodriguez Not a Typical Superstar." *Baseball Digest*, July 2000, p. 40.

37. Quoted in *People*, "The 50 Most Beautiful People in the World 1998." *People*, May 11, 1998, p. 157.

38. Quoted in Michael Knisley, "All-A-Rod, All the Time." *Sporting News*, June 28, 1999, p. 18.

39. Quoted in *People*, "The 50 Most Beautiful People in the World 1998," p. 157.

40. Quoted in Knisley, "All-A-Rod, All the Time," p. 12.

41. Quoted in Ben Walker, "Etiquette of the Beanball." *Baseball Digest*, November 1998, p. 68.

42. Mark Ribowsky, *The Complete History of the Home Run*. New York: Kensington, 2003, p. 313.

43. Quoted in Buster Olney, *The Last Night of the Yankee Dynasty*. New York: HarperCollins, 2004, p. 101.

Chapter 4: The Nation's Highest-Paid Athlete

44. Antonen, "Alex Rodriguez," p. 36.

45. Quoted in Knisley, "All-A-Rod, All the Time," p. 16.

46. Quoted in Murray Chass, "Rodriguez Strikes It Rich in Texas." *New York Times*, December 12, 2000.

47. Quoted in Jason Reid, "Texas-Sized Deal." *Los Angeles Times*, December 12, 2000, http://articles.latimes.com/2000/dec/12/sports/sp-64536.

48. Quoted in Mark Sappenfield, Todd Wilkinson, and Kris Axtman, "Enter the Era of the $49,000 at Bat." *Christian Science Monitor*, December 13, 2000, p. 1.

48. Quoted in Traina, "Timeline Alex Rodriguez."

50. Quoted in Roberts, *A-Rod*, p. 116.

51. Quoted in Traina, "Timeline Alex Rodriguez."

52. Quoted in Carlos Mendez, "Mr. Cub Anoints A-Rod as Best Shortstop Ever." *Fort Worth Star-Telegram*, September 26, 2002.

53. Quoted in *Dallas Morning News*, "Management Shares A-Rod's Pain." *Dallas Morning News*, July 16, 2002.
54. Quoted in Roberts, *A-Rod*, p. 141.
55. Quoted in Louis Berney "Living His Dream." *Hispanic*, April 2002, p. 34.
56. Quoted in Charlie Nobles, "Rodriguez Gives Miami Program a Financial Lift." *New York Times*, October 11, 2002.
57. Quoted in Tom Haudricourt, "Rodriguez Wins AL MVP." *Milwaukee Journal Sentinel*, November 17, 2003.
58. Quoted in Ken Daley, "A-Rod Says Trade Me If It Makes Rangers Better Team." *Dallas Morning News*, July 13, 2003.
59. Jon Saraceno, "Rangers' A-Rod Is in the Money but also in a Losing Proposition." *USA Today*, July 30, 2003.

Chapter 5: A New York Yankee

60. Quoted in Tyler Kepner, "Yankees Welcome Rodriguez, an M.V.P. Who Wants to Blend In." *New York Times*, February 18, 2004.
61. Quoted in Larry Stone, "Shortstop Star Power." *Baseball Digest*, May 2001, p. 34.
62. Quoted in Roberts, *A-Rod*, p. 194.
63. Norman Chad, "A-Rod Just Can't Win." *Washington Post*, October 2, 2006.
64. Joe Torre and Tom Verducci, *The Yankee Years*. New York: Doubleday, 2009, p. 241.
65. Quoted in Roberts, *A-Rod*, p. 163.
66. Torre and Verducci, *The Yankee Years*, p. 255.
67. Quoted in Joe Christensen, "Alex Rodriguez Motto—Just Relax." *Baseball Digest*, July 2007, p. 72.
68. Quoted in Anthony DiComo, "Yankees Finalize Deal with A-Rod: Reigning American League MVP Signs 10-Year Contract," MLB.com, December 13, 2007, http://newyork.yankees.mlb.com/news/article.jsp?ymd=20071213&content_id=2324707&vkey=news_nyy&fext=.jsp&c_id=nyy.
69. Quoted in *New York Times*, "Alex Rodriguez Says Claim of Infidelity Is Irrelevant." *New York Times*, August 1, 2008.
70. Quoted in Roberts, *A-Rod*, p. 2.

71. Quoted in Roberts, *A-Rod*, p. 190.
72. Alex Rodriguez, interview by Katie Couric, "A-Rod: I've Never Used Steroids," *60 Minutes*, CBS, December 16, 2007, www.cbsnews.com/stories/2007/12/13/60minutes/main3617425.shtml.

Chapter 6: Dishonor and Redemption

73. Quoted in Selena Roberts and David Epstein, "Confronting A-Rod." *Sports Illustrated*, February 16, 2009, p. 30.
74. Alex Rodriguez, interview by Peter Gammons, "Rodriguez: 'Sorry and Deeply Regretful,'" *SportsCenter*, ESPN, February 9, 2009, http://sports.espn.go.com/mlb/news/story?id=3895281.
75. Quoted in Roberts and Epstein, "Confronting A-Rod," p. 28.
76. Quoted in Tyler Kepner, "As Team Looks on, Rodriguez Details His Use of Steroids." *New York Times*, February 18, 2009.
77. Quoted in Tyler Kepner, "Rodriguez Lets His Play Define His Persona." *New York Times*, August 14, 2009.
78. Quoted in Jon Heyman, "Home Run." *Sports Illustrated*, June 1, 2009, p. 34.
79. Quoted in Jack Curry, "Rodriguez Savors a Day Out of the Harsh Spotlight." *New York Times*, August 9, 2009.
80. Quoted in Eric Neel, "A-Rod Looking Like A-Monster," ESPN, October 20, 2009, http://sports.espn.go.com/mlb/playoffs/2009/columns/story?columnist=neel_eric&id=4581610.
81. Quoted in Ron Scherer, "Alex Rodriguez Earns His Keep in Game 4 of World Series." *Christian Science Monitor*, November 2, 2009, p. 2.
82. Quoted in Tom Verducci, "Mr. November." *Sports Illustrated 2009 World Champions Commemorative*, November 2009, p. 75.
83. Quoted in Paul White, "Alex Rodriguez Back from Rock Bottom, Ready for More." *USA Today*, February 25, 2010, http://content.usatoday.com/communities/dailypitch/post/2010/02/alex-rodriguez-back-from-rock-bottom-ready-for-more/1.

84. Quoted in Ben Shpigel, "Two Will Climb Ladder, but How High?" *New York Times*, February 25, 2010.

85. Quoted in Baseball Almanac, "Alex Rodriguez Quotes," Baseball Almanac (website), www.baseball-almanac.com/quotes/alex_rodriguez_quotes.shtml.

1975

Alexander Emmanuel Rodriguez is born on July 27 in New York City.

1979

The Rodriguez family moves to the Dominican Republic, where Alex first plays baseball.

1983

The Rodriguez family moves to Miami, Florida.

1984

Rodriguez's father abandons the family and divorces Lourdes.

1992

As a high school junior, Rodriguez leads Westminster Christian School to the number-one ranking in two national polls of high school baseball teams.

1993

On June 3 the Seattle Mariners make seventeen-year-old Rodriguez the number-one choice in baseball's amateur free-agent draft; he signs with the Mariners on August 30.

1994

On July 8 eighteen-year-old Rodriguez becomes the youngest player in a decade to make a major league debut.

1998

On September 19 Rodriguez hits a home run to become the third player in major league history and the youngest to hit forty home runs and steal forty bases in one season.

2000

In December Rodriguez signs a ten-year contract with the Texas Rangers for $252 million, becoming the highest paid athlete in U.S. sports history.

2001

On September 28 Rodriguez becomes the first shortstop to hit fifty home runs in a season.

2002

On April 30 Rodriguez becomes the second youngest player to hit 250 home runs; on November 2 he marries Cynthia Scurtis.

2004

On February 16 Rodriguez is traded to the New York Yankees; on November 18 his daughter Natasha Alexander is born.

2007

On August 4 Rodriguez becomes the youngest player to hit five hundred home runs at the age of thirty-two years and eight days.

2008

On April 21 Rodriguez's second daughter, Ella Alexander, is born; in September Rodriguez and his wife, Cynthia, divorce.

2009

Rodriguez admits using performance-enhancing steroids from 2001 to 2003; he wins his first World Series.

For More Information

Books

Alex Rodriguez and Greg Brown, *Hit a Grand Slam*. Dallas, TX: Taylor Trade, 1998. A biography coauthored by Alex Rodriguez.

Selena Roberts, *A-Rod: The Many Lives of Alex Rodriguez*. New York: HarperCollins, 2009. The reporter who broke the story on Rodriguez's steroid use offers a solid biography of the player. A book for the older reader.

Wayne Stewart, *Alex Rodriguez: A Biography*. Westport, CT: Greenwood, 2007. A fact-filled biography for younger readers about Rodriguez.

Joe Torre and Tom Verducci, *The Yankee Years*. New York: Doubleday, 2009. An intriguing behind-the-scenes look at the Yankees by the team's former manager, Joe Torre. For older readers.

Jeffrey Zuehlke, *Alex Rodriguez*. Minneapolis, MN: Lerner, 2009. A biography about Alex Rodriguez for younger readers.

Internet Source

CNN.com, "Alex Rodriguez Profile," CNN.com, www.cnn.com/CNN/Programs/people/shows/rodriguez/profile.html.

Periodicals

Mel Antonen, "Alex Rodriguez: Master of Baseball Arts." *Baseball Digest*, December 2000.

Louis Berney, "Living His Dream." *Hispanic*, April 2002.

Evan Grant, "Texas' Alex Rodriguez: A Complete Package of Talent." *Baseball Digest*, March 2002.

Michael Knisley, "All-A-Rod, All the Time." *Sporting News*, June 28, 1999.

Selena Roberts and David Epstein, "Confronting A-Rod." *Sports Illustrated*, February 16, 2009.

Kelly Whiteside, "Alex Rodriguez." *Sports Illustrated*, March 22, 1993.

Websites

AROD (www.mlb.com/players/rodriguez_alex/index.jsp). This is Alex Rodriguez's official website.

Baseball-Reference.com (www.baseball-reference.com). This site includes complete major league statistics for Alex Rodriguez.

ESPN (www.espn.com). This site has stories and statistics about Alex Rodriguez.

New York Yankees (http://newyork.yankees.mlb.com/index.jsp?c_id=nyy). This is the official website of the New York Yankees. It includes articles, statistics, and a biography of Alex Rodriguez.

Picture Credits

© Andre Jenny/Alamy, 16
AP Images, 9, 13, 14, 22, 25, 30, 31, 33, 36, 38, 40, 42, 45, 47, 51, 57, 59, 62, 70, 73, 77, 80, 82, 85, 88
© Howard Harrison/Alamy, 65
© John Warburton-Lee Photography/Alamy, 28
Maryland Cartographics, 15
© PCN Photography/Alamy, 69
© Tom Tracy Photography/Alamy, 19
© Visions of America, LLC/Alamy, 54

About the Author

Michael V. Uschan has written over seventy books, including *Life of an American Soldier in Iraq*, for which he won the 2005 Council for Wisconsin Writers Juvenile Nonfiction Award. Uschan began his career as a writer and editor with United Press International, a wire service that provided stories to newspapers, radio, and television. Uschan considers writing history books a natural extension of the skills he developed in his many years as a journalist. He and his wife, Barbara, reside in the Milwaukee suburb of Franklin, Wisconsin.